Leamington's Czech Patrio..
& The Heydrich Assassination

Alan Griffin

With my thanks and best wishes

Alan Griffin

This book is dedicated to
George Pavel, Joseph Kalas
and all those brave Czechoslovaks
who fought against the tyranny of Nazism

Feldon Books

First published 2004

ISBN 0 9514478 3 1

A Cataloguing in Publication Record
for this title is available from the British Library.

Typeset in Caslon
Printed in Great Britain by
Warwick Printing Company Limited.

Contents

Front cover
Winston Churchill inspecting men of the Czechoslovak Brigade at
Moreton Paddox on 19 April 1941 [George Pavel]

Author's Acknowledgements

This book would not have been possible without the help of three former members of the Czechoslovak Army, two of whom are still living in Leamington Spa. Josef Kalas was a close friend of Jan Kubis and Josef Gabcik, the two members of the ANTHROPOID team. He slept in the same billet at Moreton Paddox and frequently shared a taxi with the two for evenings out in Leamington. Josef kept a diary throughout the five years he spent on English soil and this record has been invaluable in understanding the day-to-day life of a Czech soldier in exile. Although written entirely in Czech, the diary was diligently translated into English by another former soldier, Eric Strach, now living in Liverpool, to whom special thanks are also due. George Pavel served with Adolf Opalka another of the paratroopers commemorated on the fountain. Both were members of the Machine Gun Section based in Kineton. George has several albums of photographs and ephemera relating to the time the Czechoslovak Brigade spent in England and he has been most generous in giving me free access to these. To each of these modest and self-effacing men I offer my sincere thanks.

Jan Hyrman of the Military Society (West) in Prague volunteered his services as a picture researcher for me in the Czech Republic and I am greatly indebted to Jan for all his efforts and the considerable time that he spent in tracking down many of the photographs reproduced in this book.

I am greatly indebted to Norman Painting for writing the Foreword and I am very appreciative of his comments about the book.

Finally, my wife Lee has again been my editor of first resort and I thank her most sincerely for her support and encouragement in what is now my sixth local history book.

I also wish to place on record my appreciation for the assistance given by the following individuals and organizations:- Peter Ashley-Smith; Jenny Barnes, Heritage Interpretation Officer, Royal Pump Rooms; Richard Beith and The Czechoslovak Philatelic Society of Great Britain; Peter Bolton; Czech News Agency (CTK) Prague; Czech Army Museum, The Military Historical Institute, Prague; Mrs Dianne Crookes; Lt. Colonel Frantisek Dolezal; Richard Gaskell; Bill Gibbons; Lady Hamilton; Judith Harridge, Local Studies Librarian, Leamington Spa Library; Mrs Joan Johnson; Imperial War Museum Photographic Library; Mrs Barbara Hudecek; Major General M F Kaspar and the Association of Czech Legionnaires; Mrs Betty Kostelnik; Dr Karel Machacek; Mrs Olwen Markham; The Military Historical Society West (Prague); National Archives, Kew; Jack Pratley; Richard Phillips; Percy Russell; Robin Timmins; The Librarian Warwickshire College, Moreton Hall campus; Yivo Institute for Jewish Research, New York.

The photographs are from a number of sources which are credited in the caption which accompanies each picture.

Foreword

When, having read this book in manuscript I was enthusing about it to a friend, I was somewhat put down by the question : 'Do we need another book about the Heydrich assassination?' It set me thinking. After all, that heroic incident and the appalling atrocities including the obliteration of the village of Lidice, that followed it in reprisal are too well known. And yet I felt this book was different.

This is no tired old tale: it is a fresh account at first hand of what actually happened minute by minute. The author takes us there, we experience the tension of waiting, we not only know the names of the patriots – Jan Kubis and Josef Gabcik – but we feel in some sense that we know them. The author leads us on the escape of the patriots, from Czechoslovakia, first to France, then to Britain, and finally to Leamington, where they would stay in the town or in nearby villages for two years, absent only for brief specialized training courses.

Within a month of the Czechs departure from Leamington, Heydrich was assassinated.

I found this book vivid, well-researched, involving and above all free from sensationalism. Alan Griffin tells his story with admirable clarity in a cool direct style. It is full of anecdotes, many of them amusing and some of them revelatory, with unexpected glimpses of Robert Maxwell, Winston Churchill and Vilem Tausky among others.

For those of us who were away from Leamington during the war years it fills a gap with colour, incident and humour. To all who love Leamington and are proud of its involvement in recent history through those Czech patriots whose story is told so sympathetically here, this book will be a delight.

Do we need another book about the Heydrich assassination, about the passionate love of freedom that inspired it, and about those Czech patriots who carried it out? I think we do. This is that book.

Norman Painting

Introduction

Every year tens of thousands of people both residents and visitors walk through Leamington's Jephson Gardens to admire the floral displays or maybe just to feed the ducks on the pond. I suspect that most of them pay little attention to the stone fountain and the bronze plaque just off the main drive near to Henry Jephson's memorial. Those who stop to read the inscription are no doubt surprised to discover that the fountain commemorates one of the most daring secret operations of the Second World War.

Between 1940 and 1942 the Free Czechoslovak Army was based in mid-Warwickshire. Their headquarters were at Harrington House in Newbold Terrace just a few yards from where the fountain now stands. It was in Harrington House that Czech Military Intelligence drew up an audacious plan code named ANTHROPOID to assassinate Reinhard Heydrich, one of the most powerful men in the Third Reich, a man who was looked upon by many Nazis as the likely successor to Adolf Hitler. With the assistance of the British Special Operations Executive, SOE, men of the Czechoslovak Brigade were trained as agents and dropped by parachute into occupied Czechoslovakia. In the Spring of 1942 they accomplished their mission to assassinate Heydrich.

Since the war, Operation Anthropoid has been the subject of a number of books and several documentary and feature films. The story is nevertheless still largely unknown by many local people. It is a graphic and tragic episode which deserves re-telling. This account places the operation within the wider context of the presence in mid-Warwickshire of the Free Czech Army.

Throughout the book I have adopted the simplified form of punctuation of Czech words now commonly used. Similarly I have for the sake of readability sometimes abbreviated the word Czechoslovak to Czech. I apologize in advance to my Slovakian friends and would like to assure both them and my readers that no slur is intended.

Alan Griffin
Leamington Spa
May 2004

The Czechoslovakian soldier will never forget England or her noble people.

This beautifully painted card was made by a Czech soldier who was a patient in Warwick Hospital in November 1940. It bears the name Al Turino and was given to Elsie Atkins who may have been one of the hospital nurses. [Leamington Library]

The Czechoslovak Brigade in Warwickshire

In 1938 Czechoslovakia had a thriving democracy, the only one in Central Europe, as well as one of the largest, best trained and equipped armies in Europe. It also had an armaments industry in advance of any in the world. Czechoslovakia was at this period the world's largest exporter of arms. Hitler was acutely aware of all these facts and was swift to recognise that the Nazis' expansionist ideals would be ideally served by the annexation of the country.

Within months, twenty five German Divisions had crossed the Czechoslovak frontier to occupy the area known as the Sudetenland in which the majority of the population was German speaking. At a stroke the Germans had appropriated enough armaments to equip thirty divisions and dozens of Luftwaffe squadrons. The spoils included one thousand front-line aeroplanes, six hundred tanks, one and a half million rifles and two thousand five hundred guns of different calibres. The invasion of the whole of Czechoslovakia in March 1939 led to the formation of the German Protectorate of Bohemia and Moravia under the control of a Reichsprotektor appointed directly by Hitler.

Escape from the Nazis

Before the invasion, the President of Czechoslovakia had been Eduard Benes who had succeeded Thomas Masaryk, the 'father' of the republic on his retirement in 1935. In July 1939 Eduard Benes flew to London to establish a government-in-exile. At his first meeting with British Foreign Secretary Lord Halifax, Benes and his Defence Minister General Ingr identified as one of their primary requirements the necessity of co-ordinating the efforts of the various Czechoslovak units which had been forming in France and Poland and to a lesser degree in Britain. In October 1939 this 'Army' numbered a mere 120 men housed in a hutted camp provided by the French in the small Mediterranean town of Agde. The camp had been built originally to house refugees of the Spanish civil war. The French had issued the Czechoslovak troops with grimy, pale blue uniforms which had been lying in stores since the end of the First World War. They had no shoes, only wooden sabots, and rifles dating back to the last century which had been issued without magazines.

The ranks of this ad hoc group were swelled within a few weeks by other young men, all of whom had exciting tales to tell. Many of the troops at Agde were young men sent out of Czechoslovakia by their parents. Others like Henry Baumgarten were Jews who had the foresight to leave before Hitler's invasion. There were volunteers from a number of countries, some from England. Many had braved the border guards of several countries to join up and had trekked across Europe without passports or money in order to take up arms against the Nazis who had taken away their homeland without a shot being fired.

The risks run by the Czechoslovak volunteers were considerably greater than for most of the volunteers in the West who had merely to go to the nearest recruiting office to sign up. Many of these young men had been involved in resistance or had been identified as anti-German. If caught by the Nazis while trying to escape, they could be executed. If they succeeded in escaping, their families would be taken hostage and sent to concentration camps. Their one option to fight against the Germans was to find a recruiting office for the French Foreign Legion and to sign on with them. Four thousand places had been reserved in the Foreign Legion for the Czechs. The men signed on for a period of five years but Benes had made an agreement with the French whereby those Czechs who signed on would be released for service with the Czechoslovak army in the event of war being declared.

Josef Kalas had been a regular soldier before the occupation and soon discovered that the Gestapo were taking an interest in him. He secretly crossed into Poland and made his way to Cracow where he found other Czechoslovak army personnel crammed into the Czech Consulate. It was clear that their presence was something of an embarrassment to the Poles and they were advised not to stay. In a Baltic port they located a Polish ship about to embark on her maiden voyage to South Africa. It seemingly proved fairly easy for scores of men to 'hitch a lift' on this vessel with an instruction to the captain to put them ashore in the South of France. He duly obliged.

Young Jiri (George) Pavel was a seventeen year old student at the Textile College in Prague when he and the lad he sat next to in class made the momentous decision that they too were joining the ranks of the combatants. George had saved several weeks' pocket money and when he had finished his exams in November 1939, without saying a word to anyone, he left home. He and his friend crept out of the house at 4.00 a.m. in the morning. He was wearing low shoes and a thin gabardine raincoat. It was mid-winter and there was over a foot of snow on the Prague pavements. He had decided that he would take with him his father's Browning revolver 'just in case'. He spent many weeks trekking through occupied Central Europe in the most severe weather whilst dodging the local Police and the Germans who were everywhere. He was arrested and locked up on a number of occasions and was one day stopped and frisked by a policeman. As George stood with his arms above his head, whilst being body searched, the secreted revolver which had been stuck in his belt fell obligingly into the voluminous folds of his baggy plus fours, where it remained undetected.

George eventually arrived at the camp in Agde via Poland, Hungary, Yugoslavia, Greece, Turkey, Lebanon and Alexandria. At Agde he was one of a large number of young Czechoslovak men, all of whom were under the official age for military service. Among his colleagues at Agde were a number of men who would later be shot whilst carrying out clandestine operations. Also in the group was a lad whom George had first met on the platform at Budapest railway station a few days earlier. Known as Jan Hoch, he had been named Abraham Leib Hoch at birth. Fifty years later George would read newspaper headlines reporting how a middle-aged millionaire had fallen from a yacht in the Mediterranean in somewhat suspicious circumstances. The identity of the dead man had been confirmed as Robert Maxwell formerly known as Jan Hoch.

Hundreds of Czechoslovak Infantry had served in France and had fought the Germans in the retreat following the fall of Paris. The Czechoslovak units had lost over four hundred dead and a similar number posted missing in action. Few of the Czechs had a very high regard for the French Army or its ability to take on the Germans. In France complacency reigned. A French major at Agde told Henry Baumgarten, 'We French do not need all these foreigners to help us to fight the Germans, we are well protected by the Maginot Line.'

Within a matter of days the French had capitulated. The capitulation of France and the signing of the Armistice with the Germans had rather ominous implications for the Czechoslovaks, who were considered by Hitler's Government to be citizens of the Protectorate and, therefore, subjects of the German Reich. Many of the servicemen mobilized in France decided to stay, but a large number, in excess of four thousand, volunteered to move to Britain to continue the fight. In late June and early July 1940 and, within a month of the evacuation of the British Expeditionary Force from Dunkirk, there was an improvised withdrawal of several thousand Czechoslovak soldiers from Sète, Marseilles and other ports in the South of France. Many other groups embarked from French ports on the Atlantic coast in a variety of mainly foreign registered ships and small boats. Most of the ships leaving from the French Mediterranean ports sailed via the Straits of Gibraltar to Liverpool and ports on the Mersey.

Re-grouping at Cholmondeley

The grounds of Cholmondeley Park near Malpas in Cheshire had been requisitioned for probable occupation by Western Command and this was the place where the Czechoslovak Army was to regroup. By the time they reached England, many of the soldiers were physically exhausted by the rigours of the campaign in France. The troops marched from the docks to the railway station to entrain for their new home and were welcomed enthusiastically by local people. This encouraged the men greatly. It was soon evident that, unlike the situation in France, there was no defeatism in Britain. A large tented encampment had been set up in the park surrounding Cholmondeley Castle and here the Czechoslovak Independent Brigade Group was formed under the command of General Miroslav. The Brigade consisted of just two complete infantry battalions and a cadre of the third.

A number of problems soon manifested themselves. Among the infantry were many Communists and former International Brigade members who had served in the Spanish Civil War. These men were unhappy with their officers and with the politicians who were recognized by the allies as the government in exile. A serious situation developed and, after some discussions involving Benes himself, the 539 'mutineers' were expelled from the Czechoslovak forces with immediate effect. They were removed from the camp and handed over to the British authorities who transferred them to an internment camp in Shropshire. They were subsequently drafted into the British Army Pioneer Corps. With the removal of the group of agitators, there remained a total of 3,276 men in camp at Cholmondeley. The army continued to reorganize, and all units obtained British uniforms and serviceable vehicles, and also, to their great joy, bren-guns. These were designed in Brno in Czechoslovakia and were manufactured under licence in England by the Enfield Armament Factory from September 1937 and that is the origin of its name BRno ENfield. Many of the men themselves hailed from Brno.

LEFT. A group of young Czechoslovakian men at the camp at Agde in French Foreign Legion uniforms wearing kepis and a variety of different tunics. [George Pavel]

RIGHT. Young Czechoslovak men en route from Aleppo (Yugoslavia) to Ankara (Turkey) in a specially chartered train. This was a small part of the journey across Europe that was to end in England [George Pavel]

RIGHT. Soldiers of the Free Czech Army march along the dockside at Liverpool having just disembarked from the ships that had brought them over to England from the south of France. Summer 1940. [George Pavel]

LEFT. Czech soldiers resting on the dockside at Sete on the Mediterranean before embarking on ships that would take them to England. Many of the men had seen action in the retreat, some had been injured and most were exhausted. A French Red Cross ambulance is on hand. [George Pavel]

RIGHT. Men on board the SS *Mahomet Ali El Kebir* an Egyptian registered ship and one of a number chartered to transport the Czech troops from French ports to England in June and July 1940 [George Pavel]

After all of the men had been enrolled, it was clear that there existed a serious imbalance between the total number of officers and other ranks. There were considerably more officers available to the new Czechoslovak Brigade than there were positions to fill and there was one officer for every four other ranks. As a consequence, many officers were without assignment. This raised many problems not least of which was the question of pay for those who had held substantive rank before the war and now found themselves serving in lower ranks. These issues were partially resolved by sending a number of officers to British special instruction schools and also by sending about two hundred officers to join the Czechoslovakian Brigade that had been formed in Russia.

The Brigade had received a very warm welcome from the people of Cheshire and the troops responded by putting on a number of public displays and patriotic concerts which were well supported by local people. President Benes reviewed the troops at Cholmondeley on 26 July 1940 and on St Wenceslas Day (28 September) the Foreign Minister Jan Masaryk unveiled a memorial there commemorating the presence of the Czechoslovak forces in Cheshire.

The Cholmondeley troops never quite got to grips with the many idiosyncrasies of the English language. The pronunciation of Cholmondeley as 'Chumley' became a constant source of amusement to them. The problems of unfamiliarity with a strange language were further compounded for the Czechs on exercise in the Cheshire countryside by the total removal of all road signs. Throughout Britain, road and village signs had been taken down to confuse any German paratroopers. As a result men frequently got hopelessly lost.

The Czechs were themselves sometimes taken for spies as the fear of invasion swept the country. It soon became necessary to issue labels with 'Czechoslovakia' printed on them in red. These could be sewn onto the sleeves of battledress tunics to avoid men being summarily arrested by every well intentioned sky watcher.

Unfamiliarity with English idioms led to a rather unfortunate and oft-quoted misunderstanding during the period at Cholmondeley. Lady Lettice Cholmondeley sent an invitation requesting the pleasure of Captain Valek's company one Sunday afternoon. At 4 o'clock precisely Captain Valek arrived at the front door of Cholmondeley Castle with his company, all two hundred of them! With a degree of sang-froid that one associates with the English upper classes, Lady Lettice arranged for all of the men to be provided with milk, apples, cigarettes and biscuits and not one of them left without some refreshment.

Whilst at Cholmondeley, a Liaison Section was formed within the Brigade, staffed by British Officers, which became known as '22LHQ'. Its job was to ease relations between the Czechoslovak Brigade then being formed and the British High Command, a function which it continued to fulfil until the end of the war.

The move to Warwickshire

Although the tented town in Cholmondeley Park had afforded adequate accommodation during the warm months of Summer 1940, the onset of Autumn made a move to more permanent and comfortable quarters imperative. In early September General Miroslav accompanied by his Chief of Staff, Lt. Col Lukas and a

ABOVE. Cholmondeley Castle,
Cheshire. The Free Czech Army was
billeted in the castle grounds in the late
Summer of 1940 after their arrival from
France. [George Pavel]

ABOVE RIGHT. The Czechoslovak
Prime Minister Msgr Jan Sramek(left)
and a Czech Army Officer watch the
camp barber at work at Cholmondeley
Park. The Czech Division was stationed
at Cholmondeley prior to moving to
Leamington Spa in the Autumn of 1940
[George Pavel]

RIGHT. A Czech Army Chaplain
celebrates communion at the improvised
camp church set up in the tented town at
Cholmondeley Park, Cheshire.
[George Pavel]

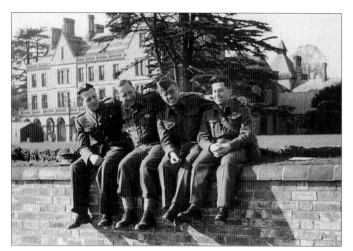

LEFT. An officer and men of the 2nd Battalion of the Czechoslovakian Brigade seated on the Ha Ha wall in front of Walton Hall c. 1942. The officers were accommodated in the Hall, other ranks were housed in temporary wooden huts in the Hall grounds. [George Pavel]

RIGHT. The building on the left is Woodley House in Warwick Road, Kineton. This was the base for the Machine Gun Company of the Czech Brigade. The officers were housed in the main building, the other ranks were accommodated in a number of temporary huts in the grounds at the back of the house. [George Pavel]

LEFT. The south front of Moreton Paddox, home of the Czechoslovak Brigade 1st Battalion. The house failed to find a buyer after the war and following a short period as a hotel was demolished. [Author's collection]

RIGHT. Moreton Hall and the surrounding estate was headquarters for the Czech Field Artillery Battery and the Transport Section. The house is now part of Warwickshire College. [Author's collection]

number of Staff Officers arrived in Leamington Spa to inspect several sites and buildings that had been identified as potential Winter quarters for the Czechoslovak Brigade. Quite what brought them to Leamington is not known. The local member of Parliament for Warwick and Leamington at that time was Anthony Eden. Since Eden was also Secretary of State for Foreign Affairs in Churchill's War Cabinet, it may have been at his instigation. In the first week of October men of the Czech Engineers Section moved into the district and began erecting temporary hutting to house the three thousand or so soldiers.

Frantisek Dolezal was one of the first Czech soldiers to set foot on the streets of the Royal Spa. Frantisek was one of about forty men sent down from Cholmondeley to help with the erection of the huts at Moreton Morrell. On his first free Saturday afternoon he and his mate decided they would go for a walk along the road to Wellesbourne. They hadn't gone very far before they met the Watkins family out in their car from Coventry to pick some blackberries. Mr Watkins was quick to volunteer the information that he had served as a Sergeant in the First World War. The men struck up an instant rapport and Frantisek and his colleague were offered a lift into Leamington. In Spencer Street the pair were dropped off but not before Mr Watkins had been into the Clifton Cinema and bought two tickets for the Czechs for the evening showing of the film.

Commencing on 13 October 1940 and over the following week in bright frosty weather the men of the Czechoslovak Brigade arrived at Leamington railway station in specially chartered trains. The Cholmondeley camp was closed.

Headquarters under Brigadier General Bedrich Neumann-Miroslav were established in Harrington House, Leamington, a large Victorian villa on the corner of Newbold Terrace and Newbold Street. The various units were dispersed to a number of requisitioned country houses to the south west of Leamington. The 1st Battalion moved into Moreton Paddox, a neo-Jacobean house with extensive formal gardens and 500 acres of park land. Moreton Paddox stood very close to another large country house, Moreton Hall, a neo-Palladian style house which had been designed by the same architect, Romaine-Walker. The Field Artillery Battery armed with 75mm French field guns, new Hillman cars and Bedford trucks moved into Moreton Hall with the Transport Section taking over the Riding School and stables. Walton Hall was also requisitioned and the elderly Lady Mordaunt found herself sharing her ancestral home with several hundred men of the Czech 2nd Battalion. The Engineers Section took over Friz Hill House on the Walton Estate and arrived in England with two pet monkeys which must have been brought over with them from France or which may have been 'liberated' on a stop-over in Gibraltar. Other units were based in and around Kineton, Butlers Marston, Wellesbourne and Barford.

Coming from a country where almost every piece of land grew crops, the soldiers were unused to seeing large tracts of grazing land. Many described the English countryside as being like one huge park. Josef Kalas was impressed with the wide streets in Leamington and the large villas which to him 'appeared like small palaces'. He had heard the saying 'An Englishman's home is his castle' and when he walked along Newbold Terrace he could see with his own eyes the 'castles' in which the English lived.

FACING PAGE TOP. The Lachine Hotel in Newbold Terrace was requisitioned for occupation by the Czech Army in 1940. The hotel was later demolished and the Magistrates' Court building erected on the site. [Bill Gibbons]

FACING PAGE BELOW. Red Cross caravans and cars parked outside 21 Newbold Terrace, Leamington the residence of Mrs MM Fowler. The Czech Brigade occupied part of the premises during the war. Mrs Fowler also owned the Blue Cafe at The Parthenon in Bath Street one of the favourite haunts of the Czech soldiers. [Bill Gibbons]

ABOVE. This large Victorian villa in Newbold Terrace, Leamington was headquarters of the Czechoslovak Brigade between 1940 and 1942. The house was demolished in the 1960's. The Spa Centre now stands on the site. [Bill Gibbons]

When the Czechoslovak Field Ambulance came to Leamington they were billeted in several houses in the Upper Parade between Warwick Street and Clarendon Avenue. The accommodation there also included a sick bay, a medical examination room and a dental surgery. Many of the men assigned to the Ambulance Unit were also musicians who made up the Brigade brass band and the choir. One of their number was a musically gifted Corporal who would become well known and much loved after the war as the conductor of the BBC Concert Orchestra on the 'Friday Night is Music Night' programme on the wireless. His name was Vilem Tausky. In his autobiography Tausky speaks of the warm welcome afforded the Czechoslovaks by the Leamington townsfolk. He also detected somewhat perceptively the underlying snobbishness that still prevailed in Leamington and the slightly patronizing hospitality offered by the town's 'upper crust' residents. He speaks quite differently about the working class people that he met, who entertained the Czech soldiers in their homes with great benevolence. What Tausky did find very disconcerting was the level of ignorance which ordinary English people displayed about his homeland. Some expressed surprise that the Czechs were not coloured. Many people thought they spoke German dialect and one soldier was asked, 'Do you have beds in Czechoslovakia?'

The men quickly settled into their new quarters and found Leamington a pleasant town with good facilities. Karel Machacek and his colleagues enjoyed strolling through the town's parks and gardens and Josef Kalas discovered to his delight that Leamington boasted no fewer than four cinemas.

The Czechs took over many of the houses in Newbold Terrace, Hamilton Terrace and the Upper Parade. The headquarters of the Brigade was in Harrington House with number 21 Newbold Terrace owned by Mrs Fowler being used to house many of the administrative and support personnel. A Field Post Office was set up at 19 Parade to handle the considerable volume of mail generated each day by the Brigade. Men attached to the Headquarters and Ambulance sections found themselves billeted in a number of town centre properties including the Lachine Hotel in Newbold Terrace and the Masonic Rooms on Willes Road. Soldiers were also billeted with local families in many of the larger town houses.

In most respects the men stationed in Leamington were better accommodated than their colleagues out in the country. Although the Brigade was in possession of some substantial and imposing country houses, these generally provided accommodation only for commissioned ranks apart from their function as administrative centres. NCO's and other ranks were quartered in standard army pattern wooden hutting erected in the grounds of the respective properties. The absence of any permanent roads and footways together with a very wet Autumn and Winter in 1940 quickly led to some of the outstations becoming seas of mud. Men continually complained of their inability to keep their boots and battledress clean and waged a constant battle to keep the mud and dirt out of their accommodation. In spite of the difficulties, the men were relieved to be in more permanent quarters after many weeks under canvas at Cholmondeley. For the first time since leaving France they were able to sleep again in proper beds.

LEFT. During the war the weekly dance at the Blue Cafe in the Parthenon in Bath Street was one of the places where young Czech soldiers went for an evening's entertainment. A number of local girls met their future husbands there. [Bill Gibbons]

RIGHT. Throughout their time in England the Czech Army operated its own field post office and distributed all its own mail. During their stay in Leamington Spa the field post office was operated from one of the buildings in the Upper Parade. This photograph shows parcels being sorted and franked for delivery. The Czech army postmark also incorporated the town's coat of arms between 1940 and 1942. [Richard Beith]

Settling down in England

Shortly after arriving in England, the Czech Government in exile had established a Cultural Department in London under the cultural attaché Dr Fischl with the express aim of showing to the British wartime public all aspects of Czech culture. Within a few weeks of settling in Warwickshire the Czechs were engaged in a wide range of cultural, sporting and educational activities. A cultural liaison office was established at the Leamington headquarters and an Anglo-Czech Friendship Club was formed in the town. A daily newspaper *Nase Noviny* (Our News) and a weekly *Prapor* (The Flag) were produced in Newbold Terrace as a means of keeping soldiers informed of current national and local news and this helped to raise morale. Although published in Czech, special English editions were produced when significant events took place.

The daily pay of a Czech soldier in England was two shillings and sixpence (12.5 p) with an additional five pence (2p) per week paid as a clothing allowance. Since board and lodgings were provided, the men had money to spend. Many of the Czechs spoke French as a second language but few knew any English when they arrived here. It soon occurred to them that the acquisition of a battery operated wireless set was an ideal way of keeping up to date with news of the war. By tuning to Radio Prague and Radio Bratislava they could also listen to concerts of Czech music and programmes in their own language. A decent radio could be bought for about five pounds and Josef Kalas was soon able to contribute thirty shillings of his savings towards the purchase of a radio by his colleagues in the Ambulance Company.

For those men 'out in the sticks' some means of transport was essential if they were to enjoy the diversions on offer in Leamington and Stratford. The ubiquitous push bike was for many the most affordable and reliable means of getting from camp into town. Henry Baumgarten and a friend in the Machine Gun Section at Kineton bought an old Austin Seven car to make sure that they didn't miss any opportunity of visiting Leamington, where, as Baumgarten admitted, 'there were many girls and great entertainment'. Petrol was of course rationed but they were always able to buy as much as they needed on the black market.

It didn't take the Czech squaddies long to track down the places around which the rather restricted social life of wartime Leamington revolved. They had soon discovered the favoured haunts of the town's womenfolk. The Assembly Room at the Pump Rooms was one such place. There was the Polka Dot cafe in Warwick Street and the Gaiety and Cadena cafes on The Parade but the big attraction was the Blue Cafe at the Parthenon in Bath Street where weekly dances were held. The YMCA Club opposite the Czech billets on the Parade was another favourite venue. The club had both upright and grand pianos which proved invaluable to Vilem Tausky and the musicians attached to the Ambulance section over the road. The Salisbury Hall in Windsor Street was opened as a service club where men could get refreshments as well as a bed for the night. There were public houses aplenty and four cinemas. All in all Leamington was an infinitely more agreeable and lively place than rural Cheshire from whence they had come.

On the evening of Saturday 19 October 1940, and just a week after arriving in Leamington, Josef Kalas was

LEFT. Josef Kalas walked back through the churchyard of Leamington parish church after his visit to the Regent cinema was interrupted by an air raid on 19 October 1940. A lady living in Church Walk died of injuries received when bombs fell in the churchyard. [Warwick County Record Office]

RIGHT. This house in Dormer Place, Leamington was destroyed on the night of the major Coventry blitz in November 1940. Two occupants of the house were killed. Eric Strach was one of the Czech medics who attended the scene to render assistance. [Warwick County Record Office]

sitting in the auditorium of the Regent cinema in Regent Grove just along from the Town Hall. Within half an hour loud explosions were heard and the whole building shook violently several times. The film stuttered to a halt and the two words AIR RAID were projected onto the screen. Josef recorded in his diary that not one member of the audience left the cinema. The equanimity of the English in moments of danger greatly impressed him. On his way home from the cinema he discovered that a number of bombs had been dropped close to the south door of the parish church leaving several large craters. Arriving back at his billets he also found that the newly acquired radio had succumbed to the recent attentions of the Luftwaffe: all the valves had been burned out.

On the 28th of October the Czechs celebrated their National Day. All of the units mustered on the lawns in the Jephson Gardens opposite the Brigade headquarters. There were speeches and celebrations and promotions were announced. All the men had to swear an oath of loyalty to the Czechoslovak army and to Czechoslovakia. To Josef Kalas the whole business reminded him of the Nazi rallies he had seen on the cinema newsreels back home before the war. Men wondered quite why they were having to swear allegiance yet again, having done so on any number of previous occasions. Surely once should be enough, they thought.

Lady Benes, wife of the Czechoslovak president, came to Leamington in early November and was welcomed by the Commander of the Ambulance Station, Dr Novotny. She presented the unit with a new ambulance vehicle which had been donated by Czechs in the United States.

She inspected the mens' accommodation and was also shown the kitchens. Much to her delight she saw there some buchty, a traditional Czech stuffed cake fresh out of the oven. The men made sure that a small parcel of the buchty went back to London with her.

The bombing of Coventry

The evening of Thursday November 14th was moonlit and frosty. At about eight o'clock the sound of anti-aircraft fire was heard. Although no one realised it at the time, this was the precursor to a night of aerial bombing, the intensity of which had not hitherto been experienced. The sound of falling bombs could be clearly heard and the news soon spread that the target of the bombers was the city of Coventry.

The flames of the burning city were clearly visible from Moreton Hall where several units of the artillery were mobilized to help with the delivery of anti-aircraft shells to the city. At nearby Butlers Marston, Josef Bartos of the Anti Tank Battery was able to read his newspaper by the light of the fires. Inevitably, when major bombing raids took place, not all of the bombs fell on their intended target. A number of bombs fell on and around the airfield at Wellesbourne and one fell in the grounds at Moreton Hall close to the Czech artillery barracks. When a stick of incendiary bombs was dropped at Top Farm, Loxley, some of the Czech infantry were sent from Walton Hall to assist the local Auxiliary Fire Service units and farmworker Dick Watkins who were trying to contain the incident. Many of the magnesium incendiary bombs had failed to ignite and were lying on the surface. The Czech troops were astonished and angered to discover that the unexploded bombs bore the legend 'Made in Czechoslovakia'. Just some of the huge quantities of armaments appropriated by the Nazis after the country was overrun in 1939.

In Leamington all hands were mobilized in the expectation of an airborne invasion by German paratroopers. Off-duty members of the Ambulance Section were issued with rifles and given duties in a local wood to look out for parachutists. It was perhaps fortunate that none were encountered since the men had not been issued with any ammunition. Medic Eric Strach could see the vivid glow in the sky and the occasional sweep of a searchlight. He heard planes passing overhead and the sound of gunfire and falling bombs. A sudden rustling in the bushes near at hand was much more disconcerting. 'That's it' he thought. Gripping his rifle ever more closely he shouted 'Halt, who goes there?' Fully expecting to be confronted by at least one German paratrooper armed to the teeth. Eric again pointed the unloaded rifle and shouted in his best German 'Halt, wer ist da?' No reply came but by the eerie glow of the distant fires Eric could just make out the head of a cow nibbling nonchalantly on some leaves.

The Czechoslovak Field Ambulance was sent in to Coventry in the early hours of Friday morning (15th) to render what assistance they could. The men were shocked and deeply moved by the whole experience. Tausky was one of those who turned out with the ambulance. Within a few days he had composed a string quartet entitled 'Coventry' which Myra Hess later included in the famous lunchtime concerts in the National Gallery in London when it was played by the Menges Quartet.

On the night of the Coventry blitz a number of stray bombs fell on Leamington. Many of the locally based units were formed into search and rescue squads. Eric Strach found himself in such a team next morning sifting through the rubble of a bombed house in Dormer Place near the town centre. Knowing that Eric was a doctor, he was called on several occasions when a casualty was unearthed in the rubble. To the question 'Is he alive Doc?' he could do no more than shake his head and pronounce life extinct. He also recalled being asked to attend an incident in Lillington where a land mine had been dropped on some residential properties. Josef Kalas went as many local people did to look at the statue of Queen Victoria outside the Town Hall which had been moved several centimetres off its pedestal as a result of the bombing.

The plight of Coventry's homeless following the air raids gave rise to many fund raising efforts in the district and the Czech units put on several concerts in the Regent cinema to raise money.

Strange food & stranger language

The Czech soldiers were not particularly enthusiastic about English food which, given the wartime restrictions, was probably less appetising than normal. That said, the Czechs soon discovered and developed a taste for that particularly English dish, fish and chips. Czech cooks did their best to provide dishes similar to those enjoyed back home. English visitors present one evening in the Mess Hall at Moreton Paddox were somewhat surprised to see with what relish the troops tucked in to a traditional supper of dumplings with cocoa powder and melted margarine.

The resourceful cooks of the 2nd Battalion at Walton Hall made a very beneficial arrangement with Roland

ABOVE LEFT. A group of Czech soldiers gathered round an army truck on the forecourt of Moreton Hall in 1941. The man standing immediately behind the officer in the leather coat is Oldrich Dvorak. Dvorak was a specialist radio operator who was parachuted into Czechoslovakia in April 1942 with a new transmitter for the Czech underground. He was shot and killed at Radocovice on 10 July 1942 after discovery of the transmitter. [Olwen Markham]

BELOW LEFT. A group of Czech Machine Gun Company soldiers in one of the accommodation huts at Woodley House, Kineton Winter 1941/1942. The man cleaning the rifle in the centre of the photograph, Franta Tomecek, was killed in the Normandy invasion. [George Pavel]

ABOVE RIGHT. A visitor inspects the hutted accommodation of the 2nd Infantry Battalion at Walton Hall. The duty roster board for the 3/2nd company has the date 11th September chalked up and the names of those detailed for cleaning and guard duties on that date. [Dianne Crookes]

BELOW RIGHT. George Pavel and fellow soldiers of the Czech Machine Gun Company gather in the yard at the back of Woodley House, Kineton prior to an exercise in 1941. Among those in the photograph are Adolf Opalka (Parachutist died in the siege of Boromejsky church), Oldrich Pechal (Parachutist executed in Mauthausen by the Gestapo), Adolf Horak (Turned Gestapo informer executed in Terezin) and Catana Klaudius (Hanged by the communists in 1948) [George Pavel]

Newman and his father, who ran a bakery in the nearby village of Wellesbourne. On one day of each week the Newmans got up rather earlier than normal to complete their own baking. As soon as they were out of the bakehouse and on their round, the Czechs moved in bringing with them all their own ingredients. If any local youngsters came into the bakehouse that day they would invariably go away with a freshly baked slice of Czech apple strudel. Any ingredients left over at the end of the day were always left in the bakery.

The influx of large numbers of military personnel into rural areas had a significant impact on many local businesses, particularly those supplying such staples of the diet as milk and bread. The extra business generated could quite easily result in a doubling of demand.

Many of the Czech units made sterling efforts to provide as much of their own food as they possibly could. Men of the Engineers Section at Friz Hill House Walton grew all their own vegetables and fattened a number of bacon and pork pigs. The Walton Estate rabbit population provided not only good sport for the local soldiery but also made a valuable addition to the men's meat ration.

The language barrier continued to present major obstacles for many of the men. An English pocket dictionary was an essential addition to what few personal possessions men were able to accumulate. Making his way to St Mary's church on Christmas Day, Josef Kalas was wished 'Happy Christmas' by his fellow church goers. He had absolutely no idea what this meant and even less idea of how to respond. To be on the safe side, he courteously bade everyone 'Good Morning'. Second

Lieutenant Silva's command of English was similarly limited. His vocabulary was mainly based, according to a fellow officer, on the word 'yes' which he used to respond to anything which he thought might be a question. Whilst staying with the Palmer family in Leamington one weekend he was asked by Mary, one of the daughters of the house, if he played the violin. He replied as always in the affirmative. To his utter confusion and embarrassment, she immediately produced a violin and a bow which she thrust into his arms. Prompted by a colleague, he managed to blurt out the words 'Oh no' accompanied by much head shaking.

A VIP visitor

In 1941 the Czech units settled down to serious training. The infantry made regular trips to the Wedgenock firing range in Warwick and all units took part in joint Western Command exercises, frequently alongside local units of the Home Guard. One of the roles of the Czechs and the other free armies based in Britain was to play the 'enemy' to test the readiness and effectiveness of the forces defending the coast. They were involved on a regular basis in mounting guard at sensitive military bases in Warwickshire. For the men of the infantry battalions that meant supplementing the guard at places such as RAF Wellesbourne Mountford, the local Operational Training Unit. They were also on occasions assigned to mount guard at the scene of RAF Wellington bomber aircraft which had crashed on take off from Wellesbourne. This was an all too common occurrence. The Wellesbourne station had lost 96 aircraft and over two hundred and fifty aircrew were killed before the war ended. On Easter Sunday 1941 the Czech soldiers were at Little Hill Farm, Wellesbourne guarding a crashed Luftwaffe aircraft. This was a

Heinkel HE111 shot down by a British night fighter during a bombing raid over Coventry. Hordes of people turned up at the scene from miles around all eager to claim a piece of the aircraft as a souvenir.

By the Spring of 1941, much had been done at each of the outstations to improve the roadways and footpaths and to generally make them more presentable. The soldiers were now properly equipped and had attained a high degree of competence and professionalism. President Benes decided that the time was ripe for him to parade his Army before the British Prime Minister.

On Saturday 19th April 1941 Winston Churchill and his wife Clemmie were driven to Moreton Paddox to inspect the Czechoslovak Brigade 1st Battalion. Also in the party with Benes were the Czech Prime Minister, Monsignor Jan Sramek, Mr Averell Harriman, President Roosevelt's personal representative, and Major General Arnold, Chief of the US Army Air Corps. This distinguished group of visitors was welcomed by General Miroslav. The Moreton troops formed up on the sports field and, as the Brigade orchestra struck up the fanfare from the opera Libuse, the inspection began. The event was well covered by staff photographers from the Czech Army Photographic Service and also by film crews for the cinema newsreels.

Churchill made a typically stirring oration which concluded with his solemn pledge that ' ..... the British Commonwealth of Nations will never weary, but will go on to fight with renewed energy, force, and courage up to the moment when the world will be a world of free men again and Czechoslovakia restored'. Not many of those present understood what had been said but their

newspaper Nase Noviny carried the full text of his speech the following week and his words were widely read and greatly acclaimed. A special English edition of the paper was also produced with a fine pen and ink drawing of Winnie filling the front page.

After taking tea in the officers' mess at Moreton Paddox, the entourage was driven the short distance to Walton Hall where the 2nd Battalion was similarly inspected. Benes gave a short patriotic speech to the assembled troops saying that, although many of them had fled from country to country, he could promise them 'this is the end, from this country you will go home'. Few of the men could have foreseen that such a day was four long years away.

As Churchill was ready to leave, the Czech Army Choir broke into Rule, Britannia. Tausky said that there were tears in the great man's eyes. To hear such a very English tune sung in vigorous Slav accents, by soldiers who could only just manage the words was a moving experience for all who heard it.

The daily routine of the troops continued very much as before with local training interspersed with exercises and manoeuvres in more distant parts of Britain. The Malvern Hills and the Brecon Beacons were frequently the location for large-scale manoeuvres, as was Cannock Chase. These exercises were not entirely without danger. In one exercise near Shelsley Beauchamp in Worcestershire, an English soldier was shot dead by one of his own side. It wasn't until news of his death reached the Czechs, who were as usual playing the 'enemy', that they also learned that the English had been using live rounds on both days of the exercise whilst they themselves had been firing only blanks.

ABOVE. The British Prime Minister Winston Churchill visited the Czech troops at Walton Hall and Moreton Paddox on 18 April 1941. In the photograph are (left to right) Mrs Churchill, Major General Arnold (Chief of US Army Air Corps), Mr Averell Harriman (President Roosevelt's personal representative), Winston Churchill, Dr Benes, Brigadier General Miroslav-Neumann and Msgr Jan Sramek (Czech Prime Minister). [IWM H8937]

Training with the Special Operations Executive

At an early stage of the war Benes had decided that the credibility of his Government-in-exile would be greatly enhanced if some covert operations could be carried out in Czechoslovakia. These would not only impede the Nazi war effort but would also serve to encourage those Czechs who made up the resistance movement.

In April 1941, Major Eric Strankmuller, deputy chief of the Czechoslovak Intelligence Service, arrived at Brigade headquarters in Leamington. He had been sent by his boss Colonel Moravec. Such a visit was unusual but Strankmuller had come with a special purpose in view.He came to ask company commanders to supply him with the names of men who they thought were suitable for special duties. The requirements were very specific. Those selected were to be brave, patriotic and intelligent. They needed to be able to keep secrets and to control their emotions under the most stressful conditions. No one with a history of drunkenness or womanising would be considered. The exact nature of their duties was not disclosed but it became clear to those seated round the table at Harrington House that Strankmuller was recruiting men to act as agents.

Within a month, headquarters were able to provide Moravec with a list of thirty six men who fulfilled all of his requirements. They were a mix of officers and NCO's. All of the volunteers were interviewed by Colonel Palacek the intelligence officer in charge of selecting agents and each was asked if he was willing to carry out covert missions in Czechoslovakia. It was stressed that these missions would be dangerous and men could opt out if they so wished. To draft men for such missions was clearly unthinkable.

On 17 July 1941 a group of eight men left their units to travel to Scotland for initial training. All were young and fit and had a good military record and none of them was married. A larger group of twenty made up a second course which began a month later on 15 August.

The month-long training courses were run by the British Special Operations Executive (SOE) who had been given responsibility for training all of the allied special agents for clandestine duties. Men were sent initially to a paramilitary training school known as STS25 near Mallaig on the west coast of Scotland for commando training. Each course was taught unarmed combat, the use of small arms, the manufacture of hand-made bombs, survival skills, map reading, concealment and a course in silent killing with Captain Bill Sykes, formerly of the Shanghai Police. The training was tough and men achieved a high level of physical fitness. At the end of the course, and without any rest or leave, they were taken to STS51 at RAF Wilmslow in Cheshire for an intensive two-week parachute course. At the end of their training, the newly qualified parachutists were returned to their units or sent to a holding centre known as STS2 at the Villa Bellasis near Dorking if an operation was imminent.

The enterprising engineers at Friz Hill constructed a practice jumping platform in the top of a large Scots Pine so that the newly trained parachutists could keep up their training. The tree was climbed by means of permanent metal and wooden spikes inserted around the trunk of the tree from ground to the top. The platform had a hatch built in of similar dimensions and design to that fitted to the bombers from which they might one day return to Czechoslovakia.

Sport & Recreation

Physical fitness had long been an important part of daily life for many of the Czechs. There was in Czechoslovakia a country-wide gymnastic association which went under the name of SOKOL. Membership of SOKOL was open to both sexes and from its foundation in the early days of the Republic it had been closely allied with the cause of Czech nationalism. When the army came to Leamington the men were eager to demonstrate their agility and physical prowess before the local townsfolk. It wasn't long before a few of the town's younger womenfolk also decided that SOKOL held more than a passing interest for them too. Within a few months, and, under the direction of Jan Koutny an avuncular Czech Warrant Officer appropriately nicknamed 'uncle', the girls had developed a well-rehearsed sequence of gymnastic movements. Rehearsing in the Salisbury Hall in Windsor Street, Bertha Corbett and Olwen Savage and her sister Dilys and the other girls in the team were soon accompanying the Czech troops to concerts the length and breadth of England. Appearing on the bill alongside the Czech Army choir and band they performed on one occasion on the stage of the Stoll Theatre in London.

At Friz Hill House the Czech Engineers made their own outdoor bowling alley on the lower lawn. The bowlers were protected from the elements by a well constructed open-sided shelter thatched with rushes from the lake at Compton Verney. The woods could be returned to the bowling end by means of a continuous sloping metal channel, something that greatly impressed the farm bailiff's youngest son Pery Russell.

LEFT. The Czech Army football Xl line up for the photographer on the Windmill Ground in Tachbrook Road, Leamington prior to the kick-off against the Norwegian Army side on 25 October 1941. Josef Kalas is 5th from the right. [Czechoslovak Ministry of Defence Archive]

RIGHT. Members of the Czech Army Sokol group giving a demonstration of their gymnastic skills on the Windmill Ground home of the Lockheed Football Club. Summer 1941. [Mrs Horswood]

LEFT. This photograph was taken in the garden of the Salisbury Hall in Windsor Street, Leamington on June 24th 1941. The girls were all members of the physical culture team and were celebrating the 44th birthday of their team leader Captain Jan Coutny ('Uncle') [Olwen Markham]

RIGHT. A group from Leamington College for Girls who trained for gymnastics with local Czech soldiers. The soldier in the photograph is Major Prokes. The photograph was taken on the front steps of the Boy's College in Binswood Avenue. [Joan Johnson]

ABOVE. Josef Kalas was born in Brno in 1912 and had served in the Czech Army before the war. He was on the Gestapo's wanted list and managed to get to Cracow in Poland where he joined the French Foreign Legion before coming to England. He served as a Sergeant with the 1st Battalion at Moreton Paddox where he shared a hut with Jan Kubis and Josef Gabcik the two men who carried out the Heydrich assassination in 1942 [Josef Kalas]

ABOVE. Captain Arnost Tomas Chlup was adjutant of the Czechoslovak 2nd Infantry Battalion quartered at Walton Hall. Arnost Chlup was a professional soldier born in Brno in 1911 and was second in-command of the 2nd Tank Brigade in the invasion of France in 1944. He ended his Army career as a Colonel.

Football also played a major part in the leisure activities of the Czechs during their time in Britain and Josef Kalas represented the Czech army a number of times. Matches were played against many of the Midlands First Division sides on their home grounds and several thousand paying spectators turned up to watch. In his diary Josef records matches against Wolves, West Bromwich Albion, Birmingham and Leicester City and other professional sides. In the Autumn of 1941 a series of inter-allied army games were played in Leamington. Teams representing the Dutch, French, Norwegian, Polish and Belgian free armies-in-exile battled it out with the Czechs on the Windmill Ground in Tachbrook Road home of the Lockheed football club. The admission charge was a shilling for members of the public and officers and sixpence for 'other ranks'. All proceeds were for the benefit of the local Czechoslovak Welfare Fund. There were may talented players in the Czech team, among whom was goalkeeper Josef Linhart, who had played for Teplitzer FC before the war and who had kept goal for the Czech national side.

Frank Vohryzek serving with the anti-tank battery at Butlers Marston organized a fencing group which was quickly added to the public relations team. The fencers took part in exhibitions throughout England and also participated in Inter-Allied Championships. On one occasion after an exhibition at the Allied Officers Club in Grosvenor House in London, Vohryzek was invited to meet a distinguished member of the audience who in his younger days had also been an accomplished fencer. The seasoned former swordsman introduced himself to Vohryzek as Winston Churchill.

The cultural liaison office in Harrington House continued to promote Czech culture to the Warwickshire public at every opportunity. There were cookery demonstrations, art exhibitions, music concerts, plays, in-store exhibitions, dances and a host of other events and functions, all carefully scheduled alongside the men's principal commitment to the military. Men arranged concert parties to entertain local groups and the Stratford Herald reported how the soldiers had provided 'capital entertainment' at the Golden Wedding party of an evacuee couple, Mr & Mrs F W Brittain in February 1941. The children of Bridge Street Methodist Church in Stratford were entertained by a Czech orchestra and conjurer at their annual tea in March 1941.

The Czechs were generally well received everywhere they went. Soldiers driving through Birmingham en route to exercises in the Black Country were showered with gifts of cigarettes, fruit and cakes by well-wishers on the top of Corporation open-topped buses.

Lighter Moments

As the presence of the Free Czech Army in England became more widely appreciated, units received many invitations from English families wishing to accommodate soldiers for a long weekend or a week's holiday. Company Commanders had to consider whether men knew sufficient English to take up such invitations. They also had to take into account the man's appearance and behaviour since he was in most respects acting as an ambassador for the Czechs. It was often the case that there were more offers than there were men to accept them. Men volunteered their names but it wasn't unknown for people to be ordered to attend when the demand for house guests exceeded the supply of available personnel. Many of those who hosted the soldiers were people of considerable wealth who lived in some style. Two men from the 1st Battalion at Moreton Paddox were royally entertained for a week by Mrs Price at Cefnaes Hall near Rhayader. Here meal times were announced by the sounding of a gong in the hall and two maids served the food on silver plates. Before leaving, a special dance had been arranged in honour of the men and they were given a standing ovation by everyone present.

By the Autumn of 1941 Britain's farmers had been encouraged to plough up land that had hitherto been permanent pasture. As a result, the increased acreage under the plough required a larger work force when the time came to harvest the crops. The military provided a large and easily mobilized pool of labour to assist in gathering the harvest. Men from the Moreton units helped out on local farms by picking potatoes and in the early Winter months when the threshing gangs came round. Farm work was very different from what they were accustomed to and the majority of the men enjoyed the work and found it rewarding.

Tuition in the English language was introduced in August 1941 and this became compulsory for officers the following month. For the first time since their arrival in England, men began to have confidence in their ability to engage the English in their native tongue. A lot of the men had forged close friendships with local girls and had of necessity acquired a smattering of English words and phrases. Some of the girls, for their part, were equally keen to learn Czech and were able to do so with the aid of books published by the Self Taught Publishing

Company in Old Bailey, London. Language problems of a slightly different sort presented themselves to Colonel Liska of the Field Artillery Regiment when King Peter of Yugoslavia paid an official visit to the unit at Moreton Paddox in the Spring of 1942. Liska was unsure how to introduce the King and the words 'your majesty' did not form part of his extensive vocabulary. The assembled troops did well to suppress their smiles when the distinguished Royal visitor was introduced to them in Czech as 'Mr King'.

Farewell to Warwickshire

By the late Spring of 1942 the immediate threat of a German invasion was past and it was deemed prudent to re-locate the Czech Division to the south coast. A farewell party was given in Leamington for the men and many hundreds of local people came to wish them good bye. The Courier newspaper ran a piece about the Czechs and the part they had played. 'We in the Midlands can feel proud of having had the honour of entertaining a section of the newly formed Czech Army in Britain. They are destined to play their part in the ensuing struggle which must end in the complete annihilation of Hitlerite Germany. They leave us with our kindest thoughts and good wishes wherever they go.' Showing the same discipline and efficiency that had characterized their stay in Warwickshire, the entire Division packed their kitbags and drove off for the Dorset town of Ilminster on 15 May.

The Czechs had by their demeanour and temperament greatly endeared themselves to the people of Warwickshire. Since their arrival almost two years before, they had made every effort to play a positive role

RIGHT. George Pavel with his wife Betty and son Christopher. George was born in Bohemia in 1922. He came to England in the evacuation form the Agde camp in France in July 1940. In England he served in the Machine Gun Company based at Woodley House in Kineton. His Company Commander was First Lieutenant Adolf Opalka one of the seven agents who died in the church siege in June 1942. George ended the war as a Tank Commander and took part in the invasion of Europe.
[George Pavel]

RIGHT. This photograph shows members of a Czech Officers Training Course which was held in Leamington during the Winter of 1940/41. In the centre of the photograph is the Commanding Officer Novotny. One of those in the photograph is Eric Strach (middle row third from the left). Eric settled in England after the war and had a successful career as a hospital Consultant in Cheshire. [Eric Strach]

in the community and to demonstrate to their hosts the richness of Czech culture. Many of the men had struck up permanent relationships with local girls which would in the fullness of time lead to marriage and over seventy Czech soldiers married local girls whilst the Army was based in Warwickshire. However for most, sadly, this would also lead to the trauma of living under an oppressive Communist regime in post-war Czechoslovakia.

Some of the men would never return home and would for ever lie in Warwickshire soil. Private Josef Hudec had been accidentally shot and killed on guard duty. Private Grunwald had committed suicide after an ill-fated affair of the heart. Captain Frantisek Dalecky shot himself one Christmas Eve after a disagreement with a fellow officer.

Within a fortnight of leaving Leamington, two of the men who had shared a billet with Josef Kalas at Moreton Paddox had stepped in front of a Mercedes staff car in a Prague suburb and had killed one of Hitler's closest confidants Reinhard Heydrich. The story of the only successful assassination of a leading Nazi during World War II is told in the second part of this book.

Operation Anthropoid – The Heydrich Assassination

The Reichsprotektor, SS Obergruppenfuehrer and General of the Police, Reinhard Heydrich arrived in Prague on 27 September 1941 and on the following morning he took up his duties. The swastika flag and the flag of the SS were hoisted over Hradcany Castle, for many centuries the seat of Czech kings.

Heydrich was one of Hitler's closest confidants and the most feared figure in occupied Europe. He had been appointed by Hitler to bring the Czechs into line and to show them who was the boss. Reinhard Heydrich had been born in 1904 and in June 1932 had founded the German Security Service (SD) which he headed. He became the 'right hand man' of the SS leader Heinrich Himmler and had been appointed head of the Security Police in 1936. He was directly responsible for the terror campaign against adversaries of the Nazis in Germany and all of the occupied territories. In 1939 he had been asked by Hitler to prepare a so-called 'final solution to the Jewish problem' and from 1941 personally supervised the creation of a system of extermination concentration camps.

The Butcher of Prague

On the day of his arrival in Prague, Heydrich declared a state of emergency and ordered the first of a long series of executions. Two senior officers of the military resistance organization, the Nation's Defence, were sentenced under martial law and executed by firing squad at Ruzyne Barracks. The executions of 69 year-old Josef Bily and Divisional General Hugo Vojta were meant to break any anti-German resistance. Bily's last words as he faced the firing squad were 'Long live the Czechoslovak Republic! Fire you dogs'.

Within a few days, the numbers of those executed increased dramatically. Heydrich's lesson to the Czechs began at the top. Prime Minister Alois Elias was arrested and sentenced to death. On the same day, Generals Mikulas, Dolezal and Oleg Svatek were executed with many others. A seemingly unstoppable avalanche of terror had begun. Over four hundred death sentences were handed down by the martial law courts. Those executed included a high proportion of ex-army officers and the nationalist intelligentsia. By the end of November 1941, upwards of four thousand people had been arrested by the Gestapo. Heydrich ordered that all those sentenced by martial law courts should be placed exclusively in the Mauthausen concentration camp in Austria. At the same time he also set up a Jewish ghetto in the old Bohemian town of Terezin (Theresienstadt) where the first prisoners arrived before the end of the year. By the end of the war thirty-two thousand deportees had died there of hunger and disease and a further eighty-seven thousand Jews had been transported to extermination camps in Poland.

In England, Benes, the exiled President, came under increasing pressure from the Allies to pursue a more active resistance policy in the occupied Protectorate. The Czechoslovak government in exile was gradually slipping into last place among the representatives of the occupied countries that were actively contributing to the defeat of Germany. Benes confided to his Head of Intelligence

Colonel Moravec that he had a plan for 'a spectacular action against the Nazis – an assassination carried out in complete secrecy by our trained paratroop commandos'. Benes consulted none of his ministers and committed none of his plans to paper. Moravec was given a verbal briefing about this planned operation which was given the code name ANTHROPOID. The target was to be Reinhard Heydrich, already christened The Butcher of Prague.

The Parachute Groups

At the beginning of October, the first successful parachute drop in Czechoslovakia took place. Corporal Frantisek Pavelka attached to the 2nd Infantry Battalion at Walton Hall was dropped in an operation code named PERCENTAGE. This single-agent mission was to take a new transmitter, spare crystals and new codes for the Czech underground. Pavelka's arrival was to be the prelude to a series of parachute drops throughout the late Autumn and Winter of 1941/42. Although he subsequently succeeded in making contact with UVOD, the Czech underground, he was captured by the Gestapo as early as 25 October and executed in Plotzensee prison in Berlin. On the same night that Pavelka was being flown out on operation PERCENTAGE, the Gestapo and its radio locating service were able to discover the one radio transmitter then in use by the Resistance to maintain contact with the Special Operations Executive in London.

These special night-time flights ferrying agents across occupied Europe were among the most dangerous missions undertaken by the RAF during World War II. The aircraft took off alone, with the prospect of ten or

ABOVE. A portrait of Reinhard Heydrich with a handwritten dedication to his deputy Karl Hermann Frank. Frank was sentenced to death for war crimes and publicly hanged in Prague on 22 May 1946. [CTK Prague]

Prag,
Hradschin mit Dom zu St. Veit u. der Hofburg.

5.

ABOVE. A pre-war photograph of central Prague showing the cathedral of St Vitus and Hradcany Castle where Heydrich's headquarters were situated. [Author's collection]

MOST SECRET.　　　　　　　　　　　　　　　　　　　　22/1/42.

OPERATION ANTHROPOID.

The operation ANTHROPOID, consisting of 2 agents was despatched by parachute on the night of 28/29th December, 1941. They carried with them a package containing two metal boxes, the contents of which are shown in the attached schedule.

The object of the operation is the assassination of Herr HEYDRICH, the German Protector in Czechoslovakia and the small box contains equipment for an attack on him in car on his way from the Castle in Prague to his office. The la rger box contains assorted equipment for alternative attacks by:-

(a) Getting into the castle,
(b) Getting into his office,
(c) Placing a bomb in his car or in his armoured
　　　railway train.
(d) Blowing up his railway train,
(e) Mining a road along which he is going to
　　　travel.
(f) Shooting him when he is appearing at some
　　　ceremony.

The time and place of this operation will be decided on the spot but the two agents concerned have been trained in all methods of assassination known to us. They intend to carry out this operation whether or not there is any opportunity of subsequent escape.

This project is not known to the Czech organisation within the Protectorate.

Herketh Prichard
　　　　Capt
　for Brigadier G. S.
　　　22 . 1 . 42

ENCL.

LEFT. This SOE internal memo marked 'Most Secret' listed the various options for assassinating Heydrich that had been discussed with the Czech Intelligence Service. [National Archives].

FACING PAGE TOP. This specially modified Mark II Handley-Page Halifax bomber L 9613 NF-V of 138 Squadron was the aircraft from which the paratroopers of groups ANTHROPOID, SILVER A and SILVER B were dropped during the night of 28/29 December 1941. Of the flight crew of eight, Ron Hockey the skipper was the only one to survive the war. [IWM R 9334]

FACING PAGE BELOW. Reinhard Heydrich arriving at Prague railway station on 20 April 1942 to accept the gift of an ambulance train presented by the Czech puppet government to Adolf Hitler on his 53rd birthday. Within a few weeks Heydrich had been assassinated in the same Mercedes staff car. [CTK Prague]

more hours of night-time flying. Search lights, anti-aircraft batteries, night-time fighter aircraft, bad weather and mechanical failures were all real dangers lying in wait.

The logistical problems associated with flying agents into the Protectorate were enormous. The range of the Whitley aircraft then available to SOE for these drops was about 1,500 miles whilst the distance from England is just about 900 miles as the crow flies with no detours. The flights could only be made at night and only in Winter when the nights were long enough to complete the mission in darkness. The weather conditions were at that time of the year at their worst. Since the pilot had to locate the drop zone visually, the flights were regulated by the cycle of the moon. Only on nights immediately before and after the full moon was night visibility good enough for the pilots to find their way. Even then the weather could interfere and there were only a few nights each month when missions could be flown.

The provision of aircraft for these clandestine operations was never a high priority for the Royal Air Force. The requirements of the bombing offensive were always paramount. The RAF allocated SOE a Special Duty squadron No 138 based initially at Newmarket. The only aircraft available to the squadron at first was the twin-engined Whitley bomber known to aircrews as the 'flying coffin'. By October 1941 the RAF reluctantly made available three modern bombers, four-engined Halifaxes, with a much longer range and superior performance to the Whitley.

The restoration of radio communications with Prague in advance of any assassination attempt became a priority following the discovery of the Czech radio transmitter. A three-man communications team code named SILVER A was given the task. On three separate occasions in November the SILVER A team was flown out to Czechoslovakia in Whitleys. All three missions had to be aborted due to inclement weather over the dropping zone and the inability of the pilot to locate the area of the drop. An eleven-hour night flight over enemy territory in the middle of winter must have been a particularly exhausting ordeal for both the agents and aircrew. Having made three such attempts in as many weeks, all concerned must have felt that fate had conspired against them. By Christmas 1941, three vital missions were piled up in England awaiting suitable aircraft and the next favourable moon phase which would occur just before the year's end.

Benes lobbied the British for the use of one of the recently introduced Halifax aircraft which would be large enough to accommodate all three groups in one go. The Air Ministry was not receptive to any of the approaches by Benes despite some pressure by Eden and Hugh Dalton the Minister for Economic Warfare. As ever, there was no question of diverting aircraft from the bomber offensive. Undaunted, Benes decided on a different tactic. He made a deal with the Poles, another exile group, whereby the Czechs would have priority on the next flight of one of 138 Squadron's long-range Halifax aircraft. Just after Christmas the moon phase and weather appeared propitious and Moravec was telephoned with the news 'It's on.'

The Agents fly out

The ANTHROPOID assassination team comprised two Warrant Officers from the Czech 1st Infantry

Battalion at Moreton Paddox near Leamington Spa. Jan Kubis and Josef Gabcik had both served as regular soldiers before the war and the two men were good friends. Both had fought together with the Czechoslovak Division in France and had followed the same route through Poland to the French Foreign Legion and finally to England. In many respects, the delays in securing an aircraft had worked to the men's advantage. The extra time had allowed them to hone their many skills and in conjunction with SOE experts to formulate a clear plan as to how Heydrich was to be killed.

In the gathering dusk of a December Sunday afternoon, the two Sergeants were collected from a safe house belonging to Czech intelligence in Stanhope Terrace, London. The men were driven down to Tangmere aerodrome in Sussex. Here they changed into specially made civilian clothes. They were issued with counterfeit identity papers in the names of Zdenek Vykocil and Otto Strnad. Each man also received five thousand marks in currency before donning his cumbersome flying suit.

Sitting on the tarmac was a Halifax NF-V L9613 of 138 Squadron specially modified for parachuting and collected only that morning from RAF Northolt by pilot Flight-Lieutenant Ron Hockey. The large parachute containers for the men's equipment were already stowed in the aircraft's bomb bay. It probably came as something of a surprise to Gabcik and Kubis when several other parachutists climbed on board. In order to maximise the full capacity of the more powerful aircraft, ANTHROPOID was joined by men comprising two other groups. There was a total of seven parachutists on board, together with a Czech dispatcher Captain Jaroslav Sustr and the eight-man flight crew with Ron Hockey as skipper. The other groups were SILVER A and SILVER B, both of which were made up principally of men attached to the 2nd Infantry Battalion at Walton Hall. Both teams had been assigned to missions involving communications. SILVER A was made up of First Lieutenant Alfred Bartos, Sergeant Josef Valcik and Lance-Corporal Jiri Potucek. SILVER B comprised Staff-Sergeant Jan Zemek and Sergeant Vladimir Skacha.

For reasons of security the men had been warned against talking to each other during the flight and they were under instructions not to discuss their missions. There is little doubt that the men knew each other well. Jan Kubis had attended the same training course as Zemek and Skacha at Morar the previous August.

At exactly 22.00 the Halifax thundered down the flare path and disappeared into the December night on a course set for the French coast and the Rhine. The aircraft would be airborne for over ten hours. Small wonder that after seven hours flying, the air gunner and crew in the nose of the aircraft complained to the skipper of the cold. At their operating height of ten thousand feet, the outside temperature was -27 degrees centigrade.

Near Darmstadt, Foxtrot Victor was trailed by two night fighters which were driven off by the Halifax air gunners. When the dropping zone was reached it was snowing heavily, there was poor visibility with 10/10ths cloud, and the moon had set. Most of the reference points below had disappeared under a blanket of snow and accurate identification of the landscape became virtually impossible. The Czech dispatcher Sustr knew the local topography well since that was his role on the mission but

ABOVE LEFT. Sergeant Jan Kubis of ANTHROPOID. It was his bomb that killed Heydrich. [CTK Prague]

ABOVE RIGHT. Sergeant Josef Gabcik of ANTHROPOID, commander of the assassination team. His sten-gun jammed at the vital moment. [CTK Prague]

BELOW LEFT. Lieutenant Adolf Opalka of OUT DISTANCE. Opalka had been based at Woodley House in Kineton [CTK Prague]

BELOW RIGHT. Sergeant Josef Valcik of SILVER A. Valcik acted as the look-out man. [CTK Prague]

he failed to recognise any features. In Czechoslovakia, air drops were always made blind, without any assistance from people on the ground providing illumination with landing lights or flares. Hockey had to drop the agents at a height of 500 feet and an airspeed no greater than 125 miles per hour. At this speed and altitude there was a very real danger of flying the aircraft into the ground.

The prevailing weather conditions contributed to the crew mistaking the city of Prague for their intended dropping point of Pilzen. At 02.24 on 29 December the two-man ANTHROPOID team jumped from the aircraft. Before he dropped through the hatch Gabcik clasped Sustr's hand and said 'Remember you will be hearing from us'. The remaining five men of SILVER A and SILVER B dropped through the hatch thirteen minutes later and Hockey banked the aircraft for the six-hour return flight to England.

As the two agents floated down in the early hours of the morning, they found themselves in an unfamiliar countryside of open fields and not in the wooded landscape they had expected and in which there would be adequate cover. Their problems were compounded when Gabcik misjudged his altitude and injured his left foot landing on the frozen ground. It soon became clear to the two men that they were nowhere near their planned landing site at Borek. As Josef Gabcik hobbled around trying to hide the voluminous parachutes in the snow, Jan Kubis made a quick reconnaissance of the area and found an allotment shed in which they managed to conceal their equipment. After sharing a tin of bully beef and some chocolate, they decided to seek out a more secure hiding place before the sun rose. They felt sure that the sound of a single, four-engined aircraft flying at low altitude in the dead of a Winter night must surely have woken people over a wide area. With the coming of daylight, the two sets of footprints radiating from the middle of the snow-covered field would tell their own story to anyone who passed that way. Near to the landing site, the two men came across an old stone quarry in which were a number of long cave-like galleries from which stone had been extracted at some time in the past. In these abandoned workings the men went to ground.

Help from the Resistance

A local game keeper, Antonin Sedlacek, had been wakened by the sound of the low-flying Halifax and he felt sure that it could mean only one thing, parachutists. At first light he set off on his rounds to check his birds and soon found the buried parachutes and equipment. Following the footprints in the snow quickly led him to the quarry where Josef and Jan were standing outside the cavern surveying the local topography. Sedlacek came straight to the point with the two men. He told them that he had found their hidden parachutes and he also informed them that that they were near the village of Nehvizdy and only twelve miles from Prague. With Gabcik injured, and the team cut off from their contact addresses in Pilzen seventy or so miles away, the options for the two men were severely limited. They admitted to Sedlacek that they were in fact parachutists from England and asked him for help. He offered to bring food to the quarry and to find out if their arrival had been noticed by anyone else. The future of ANTHROPOID hung in the balance and rested almost entirely on the co-operation of a complete stranger who for all they knew might have been a Gestapo informer.

ABOVE LEFT. Sergeant Jaroslav Svarc of TIN whose mission was to assassinate Emanuel Moravec the Propaganda Minister. [CTK Prague]

ABOVE RIGHT. Sergeant Josef Bublik of the BIOSCOPE team. [CTK Prague]

BELOW RIGHT. Sergeant Jan Hruby of BIOSCOPE dropped on 27/28 April 1942 to sabotage railway and electrical installations. Before their departure from England each of the Czech parachutists was photographed in front of the same section of brick wall at Porchester Gate in London. The wall and the building which housed the Command Section of Special Group D is still standing [CTK Prague]

Within a few hours, the men in the quarry also received a visit from another local man whose sleep had been disturbed by the noise of the circling Halifax. Bratislav Bauman was a local miller but what was of much greater interest to the Czech agents was his avowed membership of the SOKOL sports organization dedicated to Czech nationalism. SOKOL had been a proscribed organization since October 1941 and Bauman offered to put the agents in contact with an underground group in Prague. The two discussed the proposition which ran counter to the rules that London had drawn up before the mission, banning any contact with resistance groups until the assignment had been carried out. They would be much safer in a large city and in any event Josef Gabcik would need some medical attention and time for his injured foot to heal. The two agreed to let Bauman make whatever arrangements he could to ensure their safety. With help from members of the local resistance movement, the ANTHROPOID team arrived in Prague by train early in the new year. Their equipment was collected from the quarry at Nehvizdy and gradually relocated to various hiding places around the capital.

In Prague the ANTHROPOID team was taken under the wing of the JINDRA underground organization, headed by Ladislav Vanek a former chemistry teacher and SOKOL official from Brno who had been on the run from the Gestapo for many months. Vanek's immediate concern was that the two men were German plants sent to infiltrate his organization. Having satisfied himself on that score, Vanek placed the men in the care of Jan Zelenka another former teacher and Czech Intelligence Service officer whose cover name was UNCLE HAJSKY. Zelenka's role in the underground movement was to provide safe houses and false documents for anyone who might need them. He arranged for the Agents to move into an apartment on Biskupcova Street in the Zizkov district of Prague. The flat was the home of a middle-aged railway man Alois Moravec and his wife and twenty-one year old son Ata. Here the men stayed for several weeks in great secrecy, sleeping with loaded pistols under their pillows just in case the Gestapo might call one night. When asked what their mission was, they would laugh and say 'We're counting the ducks on the Vltava river.'

None of the three teams parachuted in by Hockey in December had been able to make contact with each other. During March and April a further seventeen men were flown out and parachuted in for a variety of missions. It had been agreed that the small ads. columns of the Narodni Politika newspaper should be used as the means whereby the various teams and individuals made contact with each other. The different teams used a variety of small advertisements. These were usually concerned with the purchase of dictionaries, encyclopaedias and musical instruments. Josef Valcik of the SILVER A team had established himself as a barman at the Veselka Hotel in Pardubice, fifty-odd miles east of Prague, an ideal place to gather information as it was frequented by high-ranking German officers. By means of the small ads columns, Valcik was able to make contact with the ANTHROPOID men. His radio operator Alfred Bartos was able to inform London that the two agents were safe. Unknown to Valcik, his cover at the hotel had been blown and his description had been circulated to every police post in the Protectorate. Under orders from Bartos, Valcik took refuge in a JINDRA safe house in Prague. He dyed his hair and grew a small moustache to change his appearance. The two-man assassination squad had recruited, somewhat unexpectedly, a third member.

One of the mission objectives of the paratroopers was to assist the RAF in its attempts to bomb the large Skoda works in Pilzen which was a major supplier of armaments to the Third Reich. The target was at the limit of the range for the bomber aircraft then available to the RAF. Four unsuccessful attempts to bomb this target were made between October 1940 and October 1941. A new attempt was made on the night of 25/26 April 1942 under the code name CANONBURY. At six pm, the Czech Service of the BBC broadcast a password which was the signal for the members of airdrops, OUT DISTANCE, ANTHROPOID and SILVER A to mark the target by setting fire to ricks near the factory. The fires were set at great risk by Bartos, Opalka, Gabcik, Kubis and Valcik. Six, Short Sterling Mk 1 bombers of 218 Squadron were able to locate the target but low cloud and poor visibility meant that their bombs were dropped blind. Not a single bomb fell on the factory and the operation was a failure.

Refining the plan

The paratroopers had devised a number of plans for the assassination of Heydrich. At the beginning of April 1942 Heydrich himself contributed to the available options by moving from his temporary quarters in Prague Castle to an imposing country chateau in Panenske Brezany, a village fifteen miles north of Prague. The ANTHROPOID team spent many days working out Heydrich's daily timetable. It was soon established that he commuted each day from the chateau to his office in Hradcany Castle. The journey was made in a black Mercedes-Benz 320 open-top tourer. He was always driven by SS Oberscharfuehrer Johannes Klein, his personal driver, who collected him at nine o'clock. The total journey time to Prague was forty-five minutes. Two aspects of the journey were of particular interest to Kubis and Gabcik. They noticed that Heydrich always rode in the front of the car seated alongside Klein and only on very rare occasions was the vehicle accompanied by any form of escort. What Jan and Josef had yet to determine was exactly where on the route they would lay the ambush. They acquired bicycles and spent many days pedalling along the route. Many possibilities were considered and rejected. The single major problem was how the ANTHROPOID team were to escape following the killing.

As the men were returning to Prague one Spring afternoon they came upon the perfect location. They were descending the Kirchmayerstrasse in the northern suburb of Holesovice and noticed that there was a point where the cobbled road turned sharply right as it dropped down to the river. Although the road was wide, there was effectively a hairpin bend at this point. They got off their bikes and watched as the traffic slowed down to a crawl to negotiate the bend. The occupying Germans had with typical Teutonic efficiency recently changed the road priorities so that all traffic now drove on the right of the road as in the fatherland. This would mean that the Reichsprotektor's Mercedes would be close to the kerb at this point. Tram lines ran up the centre of the road and there was a tram stop at which the men could await the arrival of their quarry without arousing undue suspicion. Yes, this was the ideal place.

Apart from their own intelligence gathering, the ANTHROPOID team had also cultivated a number of

ABOVE. The scene of the crime with the damaged
Mercedes and the twin-car tram still in position
on the bend in the road. Gestapo agents reconstruct
the assassination. [CTK Prague]

FACING PAGE. After the assassination the
Gestapo circulated many thousands of multi-page
posters showing items recovered from the scene.
Among the items were two brief cases, the
bicycle on which Josef Gabcik had planned to
escape and Jan Kubis's unused bomb. [National
Archives, Kew]

III. Aktentasche Nr. 1.

IV. Aktentasche Nr. 2.

V. Sprengkörper.

VI. Fahrrad.

contacts inside Heydrich's headquarters in the castle. The Nazis employed Czech domestic staff who were treated as part of the furniture and who were never considered to pose a security risk. One such employee was Josef Novotny, a watch maker, who was responsible for the castle clocks. He also repaired clocks and watches for the German garrison in Prague and in consequence was able to pick up a lot of invaluable information and news. Towards the end of May, Novotny heard a rumour that Heydrich was to be moved to another post and would be flying to Berlin for a meeting with Hitler on 27 May. Heydrich had his own private Junkers aircraft permanently parked on the tarmac at Prague airport for immediate use. The rumour was that he would not be returning to Prague. If he was to be killed, the assassination would have to take place on that date, when thanks to Novotny, his movements were known. Thus was the die cast. Final approval was radioed from London to Prague on 20 May. The assassination would take place on 27 May.

The three Sergeants were joined by Lieutenant Adolf Opalka who had served with the Machine Gun Section at Kineton and had been dropped by parachute on 28 March as one of the three-man OUT DISTANCE group. After the drop, one of the team Corporal Ivan Kolarik, was tracked down by the Gestapo and had committed suicide to save his relatives from retribution. The third member of the group Sergeant Karel Curda had served with Kolarik at Moreton Hall and he and Opalka, his commanding officer, made their way separately to Prague and to safe houses arranged by the JINDRA organization. Gabcik, Kubis, Valcik and Opalka now made up the team which would carry out the assassination and the final preparations were put in place.

The plan was probably worked out by Gabcik. Valcik was to stand on the pavement up hill of the bend in the road and would signal with a small hand mirror to warn of the approach of the Mercedes. Gabcik would be positioned on the apex of the bend close to the kerb and would carry out the killing with a sten gun which would be hidden under a raincoat carried on his arm. Kubis would be a few yards further down the road as a reserve and would toss specially made anti-tank grenades into the car if it was still in motion. He would also grab Heydrich's briefcase after the assassination. Lieutenant Opalka was the senior officer of the team and would keep a lookout from the opposite side of the road and would assist if necessary. Both Kubis and Gabcik would have old leather briefcases in which to carry small arms and grenades and both men would have a bicycle on which they would effect their escape.

The fateful day

At 08.00 on the morning of 27 May the two men left their safe house. It was a bright Spring morning ideal for their purpose. The sten gun was broken down into its three component parts and placed in one of the briefcases. The impact bombs were placed in the other. The various weapons were hidden under layers of grass to camouflage them in the event of any casual Police checks. Many Czechs kept rabbits for food and it was quite common for office workers to collect grass for them from local parks. Both men carried .32 calibre Colt semi-automatic pistols. They caught the tram to the suburb of Zizkov and got off there where they collected their bicycles. The briefcases were strapped to the handlebars. By 09.00 the four men met at Holesovice and after propping the bicycles against lamp posts on the far side of the road, they took up their positions to await the arrival of the staff car with its distinctive SS3 licence plates. Josef Gabcik took the sten gun from his briefcase and assembled it by touch under the raincoat draped over his arm. The black Mercedes would normally pass their position at about a quarter to ten. Time dragged and number 3 and 14 twin-car trams ground their way up and down the steep slope stopping to set down and pick up passengers from the nearby stop. The possibility of passers-by getting caught up in the operation had been discussed and it was agreed that this was a risk that had to be taken.

As the minutes ticked by with no sign of Heydrich, doubts began to creep into the minds of the ANTHROPOID team. Perhaps on this day of all days there had been some last minute alteration to the route or to the timetable. This would be their last opportunity of killing Heydrich. He had never before been so late. Still the time dragged by and the nervous wait continued. Church clocks struck ten and then chimed again for the quarter and still there was no sign of the Mercedes. When the clocks chimed for half past ten, the tension became almost tangible. Quite suddenly, the waiting men caught the unmistakable flash of Valcik's mirror. Their target was on his way. It was 10.32.

Josef Gabcik released the safety catch on the sten gun still hidden beneath the raincoat and moved over to the edge of the pavement. Jan Kubis took out one of the cylindrical grenades from his briefcase. In a matter of seconds the car would be passing within a few feet of them. To his dismay, Adolf Opalka saw out of the corner of his eye a number 3 tram pull away from the stop at the bottom of the hill and begin its laborious way up the slope. The possibility was that it would reach them at exactly the same moment as their target.

As the Mercedes rounded the bend, Josef Gabcik threw down the raincoat and raised the gun to his shoulder. Taking careful aim at the front seat passenger he pulled the trigger. Nothing happened. Total silence. The gun had failed to fire. Jan Kubis watched in stunned amazement as the car passed Gabcik without a shot being fired. Instinctively he hurled the bomb into the front seats of the car. Instead of landing in the car the grenade exploded on the running board bursting a rear tyre and blowing a large hole in the bodywork. In the same instant he felt splinters strike his face and chest. Suddenly, all hell broke loose. Heydrich and Klein emerged from the damaged car brandishing their Walther pistols, both seemingly unhurt. The tram, its windows shattered, disgorged its screaming and shouting passengers into the roadway. Jan ran across the road weaving between the shocked passengers and mounted his bicycle. Pedalling furiously he had soon disappeared from view.

Josef Gabcik had been momentarily transfixed by the failure of his sten gun. The explosion of Jan's grenade returned him quickly to reality. Unable to reach his own bicycle, he threw down the gun and set off on foot pursued by Heydrich and Klein. A wild-west-style shoot out then ensued. Josef took temporary refuge in a small butchers shop. Unluckily for him the owner Brauer turned out to be a Nazi sympathiser who immediately went out into the street to indicate to the SS men where Josef was. Only then did Josef's luck change for the better. Klein's pistol suddenly jammed and, as he barged his way into the shop, Gabcik shot him in the leg. Josef vaulted over the prostrate figure of the huge SS man slumped in the doorway and ran for his life. He disappeared into the Prague side streets and didn't stop running until he got to the front door of number 1718 Kolinska Street, a safe house where Petr Fafek lived with his wife and two daughters.

At the scene of the attack confusion reigned. Heydrich looked decidedly pallid and was obviously in considerable pain. A Czech policeman flagged down a passing confectionery salesman and ordered him to unload the vehicle and take the wounded Heydrich to hospital. While driver Karel Duben was thus engaged, a van approached. This was commandeered by a blonde German woman who had been one of the passengers on the tram. The van was loaded with crates of floor polish. The Reichsprotektor was bundled somewhat unceremoniously into the back of the van amongst the tins of polish and the most powerful man in Czechoslovakia was conveyed to Bulovka hospital.

At Bulovka, Heydrich was seen by the German Director of the hospital Dr Dick. The prognosis seemed to be good. Although the bomb had seriously injured Heydrich, the vital organs were not thought to be damaged. Dick thought the wound was superficial. An X-ray however revealed a far more serious and potentially life-threatening situation. One of Heydrich's ribs was found to be fractured and fragments of horsehair and wire from the car's upholstery had been driven upwards into his spleen. An immediate operation was deemed necessary and the top Nazi consultant in Prague, Professor Hollbaum of the German Clinic was summoned to carry out the surgery.

Into hiding

Hitler was in East Prussia when he was informed of the attack just after midday. He flew into a great rage when told that Heydrich had been travelling without an escort. A reward of one million marks was immediately offered for the arrest of those who had made the attempt on Heydrich's life. Anyone caught helping the assassins was to be shot along with their entire family. Ten thousand Czechs were to be taken hostage and executed. Karl Hermann Frank the Nazi Secretary of State was placed in charge of the Protectorate. Frank proclaimed a State of Siege throughout the country and twenty one thousand troops began a dragnet operation in Prague in a determined effort to flush out the attackers.

The men of the ANTHROPOID team were by this time taking refuge in a number of safe houses occupied by members of the JINDRA group. Adolf Opalka was lodged with Mrs Tereza Kasperova and had a narrow escape. When the Gestapo arrived to carry out a search of the house Opalka had just enough time to hide in a small broom cupboard behind a sofa. Fortunately for him the sofa was not moved. Karel Curda had an even closer call and spent several minutes hanging by his fingertips from an upstairs bathroom window above a light well.

The day after the assassination attempt the Gestapo had recovered the articles left at the scene and after minute examination the various items were put on display in the window of a BATA shoe shop in Wenceslas Square in central Prague. There was the ladies' bicycle with the briefcase still strapped to the handlebars on which Josef had intended to make his escape. Inside the briefcase was an unfused bomb and a magazine for a Sten gun. Also displayed were the raincoat which he had used to conceal the gun. Another briefcase containing a primed grenade and a cloth cap had been picked up in a nearby

ABOVE. The wrecked Mercedes with the passenger door blown off photographed a few hours after the assassination. [CTK Prague]

RIGHT. A Gestapo photograph showing the blown rear tyre of the car and damage to the running board and the passenger side of the vehicle. [CTK Prague]

street and these were also displayed in the window. A large notice announced a reward of ten million crowns to anyone who might recognize any of the items on display.

It was clear to those running the JINDRA organization that the continued presence of the parachutists in safe houses might endanger not only the families of those who were sheltering them but also the organization itself. With tight security and strict controls over road and rail links into and out of Prague, any attempt to leave the city would be ill advised. It was underground leader 'Uncle Hajsky' (Zelenka) who came up with a solution. He arranged to hide the parachutists in the crypt of the Karel Boromejsky Greek Orthodox church on Resslova Street. The lay priest there, Vladimir Petrek, agreed to shelter the men and his bishop Gorazd gave his official blessing to the arrangement. The church staff and congregation were sworn to secrecy and in ones and twos Zelenka began to smuggle the agents into the catacombs under the church. Along with the ANTHROPOID team in the crypt there were several other parachutists who had been dropped in the preceding weeks. Sergeant Jaroslav Svarc was half of a two-man team dropped on 29/30 April in what had turned out to be an abortive attempt to assassinate Moravec the Education and Propaganda Minister. Also in the church were Sergeants Josef Bublik and Jan Hruby who had been dropped the night before Svarc to sabotage the railway bridge at Hradnice. The seven men settled into their new home in the dark and airless confines of the crypt. It was necessary to remove the bones of long-dead priests from the coffin niches in the walls of the crypt so that the men would have a protected place in which to lie down and sleep. They hoped to get away from Prague as soon as the heat died down.

A funeral and a betrayal

At the Bulovka hospital, Heydrich received a constant stream of black-uniformed SS men bearing flowers. Himmler telephoned hourly for bulletins to keep Hitler informed as to the patient's condition. The news was not good. Heydrich's condition deteriorated. He had developed peritonitis and shortly afterwards septicaemia was diagnosed. At 4.30 on the morning of 4 June Heydrich died. A junior clerk made a brief entry in the hospital death register. Against the name of Reinhard Tristan Eugen Heydrich under cause of death were written just two words 'wound infection'.

The Nazis, who were practised in mounting huge displays, orchestrated particularly grandiose and nauseating funeral rites for the Reichsprotektor. The spectacle had been organized by a committee headed by the Nazi Propaganda Minister, Josef Goebbels and was the grandest of any funeral ceremony conducted during the Third Reich. After two days lying-in-state in Prague, the coffin was conveyed through the city on a gun carriage to the railway station. Czech Prime Minister Hacha and the members of the puppet government accompanied the coffin to Berlin where a State funeral was held in the Mosaic Hall of the new Reichschancellery on 9 June. Himmler gave the oration eulogising Heydrich and saying that his name would live for ever as an example of duty to the Fuhrer and the fatherland. Hitler himself was too upset to utter more than a few words and to pat Heydrich's two small sons on the cheeks rather absentmindedly.

Two weeks passed and, in spite of the huge rewards offered, no one had come forward with any credible information about who the assassins were. Heinz Von

RIGHT. Karel Curda the parachutist who betrayed his comrades and informed the Gestapo identifies their bodies on the pavement outside the church. [CTK Prague]

LEFT. This photograph taken in the crypt of the Karel Boromejsky church some years after the war shows the coffin niches in which the men took refuge each night. [CTK Prague]

Pannwitz, the head of the anti-sabotage section of the Prague Gestapo came up with a different idea. He persuaded Frank that what was needed was an amnesty whereby anyone who was prepared to provide information which led to an arrest would be granted immunity by the Nazis from action of any sort. Within three days more than two thousand statements by Czechs arrived at Gestapo headquarters. Among this huge pile of correspondence was an anonymous letter telling the Gestapo that their search for the killers was at an end. The letter went on 'The perpetrators of the assassination are a certain Gabcik from Slovakia and Jan Kubis, whose brother is an inn-keeper from Moravia'. On 16 June 1942 the author of the anonymous letter walked through the doors of Gestapo headquarters at the Petscek Palace. He could tell them all they needed to know about the Heydrich assassination and operation ANTHROPOID. And how was it, he was asked, that he was privy to this information? 'My name is Karel Curda' he said. 'I am one of the Czech parachutists'. Thus was the fate of the seven men in the crypt on Resslova Street sealed. They had been betrayed by one of their own.

Karel Curda did not know where the parachutists were hiding but he knew the addresses of many of the safe houses used by the JINDRA group. One of the Gestapo's first calls was at the flat of Alois Moravec in Biskupcova Street where Jan and Josef had stayed in the early weeks. As the Gestapo prepared to take the family away, Mrs Moravec made an excuse to visit the lavatory where she locked herself in and swallowed a cyanide capsule. She was dead by the time a doctor arrived. Her husband and son Ata were arrested. Later the same day, UNCLE HAJSKY (Zelenka) who lived in the same street also received a visit from the Gestapo. He too committed suicide as his front door was broken down. Young Ata Moravec was taken to the Gestapo headquarters and tortured for twenty four hours at the end of which alcohol was forced down his throat. In a stupefied state he was presented with his mother's head floating in a fish tank. Only then did he reveal to his captors something that his mother had said to him on a number of occasions 'If you are ever in trouble Ata, go to the catacombs of the Boromejsky church.'

No surrender

As the first grey streaks of daylight lit the windows of the church on 18 June 1942, seven hundred Waffen SS troops in full battle order cordoned off the area around Karel Boromejsky. The janitor unlocked the church at 04.30 and a Gestapo detail entered the nave. They soon discovered that some of the parachutists had taken up positions in the choir loft above the rood screen when a hand grenade came bouncing down the narrow stairs. A force of Waffen SS troops was called up with strict instructions from the Gestapo to capture the parachutists alive. It took over two hours for the SS to storm the loft using small arms and hand grenades. It was seven o'clock before the firing ceased. The troops discovered the bodies of two parachutists who had taken poison and a third who was unconscious and died within a few minutes of arriving at a hospital. This was Jan Kubis. The other two agents were identified as Adolf Opalka of the OUT DISTANCE team and Josef Bublik of BIOSCOPE.

The Germans suspected that there were other parachutists in the church and Vladimir Petrek the priest admitted that there were four more men hiding in the catacombs. Having recovered three corpses, the Gestapo were very keen to capture the remaining parachutists alive. What they and the SS most earnestly wanted was someone to stand in the dock at a big show trial. Exhortation was their first tactic. Loudspeaker announcements were made promising the men that they would be treated as Prisoners of War if they surrendered peacefully. Petrek was sent up to a small grille near the pavement to speak to the men in the crypt below. Karel Curda, their former colleague and betrayer, was brought to the church in handcuffs and called out 'Surrender boys, everything will be all right'. The trapped men gave absolutely no indication that surrender was a likely outcome and a long siege began. An attempt was made to flood the crypt. The Prague Fire Brigade was summoned and the reluctant firemen were ordered to pump tens of thousands of gallons of water into the building. Tear gas and grenades were thrown down the small access shaft. The parachutists responded with a burst of gunfire.

As the day wore on with no sign of surrender, the Waffen SS commander decided that the Gestapo's wish to capture the men alive was no longer a realistic option. The decision was made that the crypt would be stormed by SS troops. Explosives were used to blast a hole in the floor of the nave and a combat detachment stood ready to enter the crypt with grenades. It was now midday. As the SS soldiers prepared to enter the flooded, gas-filled crypt, four isolated shots rang out below them. After that, a great silence. A soldier was lowered somewhat apprehensively into the hole. A few moments later he reappeared shouting 'Fertig' (finished).

The Nazis dragged the four bodies out and threw them down on the pavement in the noon sun. All were soaking wet and covered in blood. Curda the informer stepped forward to identify the bodies. Lying side-by-side were Josef Gabcik, Josef Valcik, the look-out man, and Jan Hruby and Josef Bublik of the BIOSCOPE group. The men had resisted the combined efforts of a huge force of SS troops for over six hours. Each had committed suicide with his last bullet.

While the SS men and Gestapo at the scene were still contemplating the events of the morning, an urgent message arrived from Himmler. The text read 'Any means should be employed to reassure the assassins in order to capture them alive.'

The retribution

The wave of German vengeance began the moment Jan Kubis hurled his grenade. Scores of civilians were arrested and tortured in an attempt to gain information. Three days after the attack, Josef Bartos of SILVER A was tracked down in Pardubice and fatally wounded after a gun fight with the Gestapo. Jiri Potucek, the group's radio operator, was shot dead by Czech police on 2 July. The Gestapo learned that SILVER A's transmitter had been operated from the engine room of a quarry near the village of Lezaky. On 24 June all the 57 adult inhabitants of Lezaky were taken away and executed. The children were also taken and only two sisters survived the war.

The small Czech village of Lidice was also chosen to atone for Heydrich's death. At dawn on 10 June 1942, German police surrounded the village six miles north-west of Prague. All of the 104 children were taken from their parents and sent to Germany for 'Germanification', 82 of them were murdered by the exhaust gases of specially modified trucks in the extermination camp at Chelmo on Ner. The women of Lidice were transported to the

LEFT. This photograph of the church on Resslova Street was taken on the morning of 18 June 1942 after the ending of the siege. [CTK Prague]

RIGHT. The trial of four Greek Orthodox Church officials charged with abetting the assassination of Heydrich was held in the Prague Gestapo headquarters at the Petschek Palace on 3 September 1942. All were executed. (Left to right) Jan Sonnevend (Chairman of the council of elders), Jan Cikl (Minister), Vladimir Petrek (Curate) and Bishop Gorazd. [CTK Prague]

LEFT. The village of Lidice photographed before the war. As a reprisal for the assassination of Reinhard Heydrich, Hitler ordered the execution of all the male inhabitants and the transportation to concentration camps of all the women and children. The village was then completely destroyed so that nothing of it remained. The destruction involved twenty thousand man hours. [IWM HU 47402]

RIGHT. All 173 men and boys in the Czech village of Lidice were lined up in the village street and shot. The Germans placed a row of straw mattresses up against the wall to prevent any of the execution squad being injured by bullets which might ricochet. The womenfolk were transported to the concentration camps at Ravensbruck, Auschwitz and Mauthausen where they were all executed. [CTK Prague]

Ravensbruck concentration camp where 53 of them perished. The village men who numbered 173 were lined up in the courtyard of Horak's farm and in groups of five they were summarily executed by firing squad. The whole village was then dynamited and the buildings razed to the ground. In excess of twenty thousand man-hours were expended in removing every trace of the village. The coffins in the village cemetery were dug up and a stream that had run through the village was re-routed. The name Lidice had been removed from the map. Show trials were held in Prague and Vladimir Petrek the priest from the Boromejsky church, Bishop Gorazd and two other representatives of the Greek Orthodox church were executed for co-operating in the hiding of the paratroopers.

Later the same month, the Germans had succeeded in rounding up almost three hundred Czechs from all over the Protectorate who had connections of any sort with the parachutists. This group was called the 'paratroopers group' by the other prisoners and included entire families and all the living relatives of Kubis and Valcik. Adolf Opalka's father and an elderly aunt were arrested. After being imprisoned in Terezin, they were transported in railway trucks to Mauthausen. In an October blizzard they were marched the three miles from the railway station to the camp. The SS made sure that every prisoner was dressed in light Summer clothing. Throughout the following day, 257 collaborators of the paratroopers were murdered in Mauthausen by a shot in the back of the head.

In the months following Heydrich's assassination the martial law tribunal in Prague condemned 448 people to death. At the same time the tribunal in Brno condemned to death a further 257 people. On three successive days in June 1942 three thousand citizens of Jewish origin were

ABOVE. The Mayor of Leamington, Alderman Miss Rene England at the unveiling of the Czech memorial fountain in the Jephson Gardens on Saturday 26 October 1968. The fountain was designed by John French a local sculptor and was sponsored by the Association of Czech Legionaries. [Bill Gibbons]

shipped in three transports to extermination camps where they were murdered.

The ashes of thousands of Nazi victims ended up on a rubbish tip next to the Mauthausen concentration camp. This was the final resting place of most of the Czech patriots, without whom the assassination of Reinhard Heydrich would not have been realized.

In the Jephson Gardens in Leamington there is a stone fountain in the shape of an open parachute around which are inscribed the names of the seven parachutists who perished in the church crypt on Resslova Street. Close by is a bronze memorial plaque which bears the following words.

> In tribute to all Czechoslovak soldiers,
> airmen and patriots who fell in World War II.
> From Royal Leamington Spa, in 1941
> volunteers from the Free Czechoslovak Forces
> stationed in the town were parachuted into
> their homeland to rid it of the tyrant
> 'Protektor' SS General Heydrich.
> Two of them – Jan Kubis and Josef Gabcik
> accomplished their mission in May 1942.
> They and their companions laid down their lives for freedom.

Sixty years on, a dwindling group of elderly Czechoslovak Legionnaires still gather at the fountain on June 18th each year on the anniversary of the storming of the crypt. The names inscribed on the fountain are the names of men they knew and valued as friends, men who themselves had once walked in this same park on bright Spring mornings.

The Karel Boromejsky church in Prague is now the Orthodox Cathedral of Saints Cyril and Methodius and part of the National Memorial to the Victims of the Heydrich Terror and a place of reconciliation. A bronze memorial plaque on the bullet-marked exterior wall of the church displays the names of the seven parachutists and the nine members of the church congregation who were executed for sheltering them. In 1992 Vaclav Havel the President of the Czech Republic visited the Cathedral and gave a brief address. In his speech he had this to say about the events of Spring 1942:-

'We know the price we paid for that assassination … freedom is something which has to be paid for … The assassination showed the whole world that we saw ourselves as a subjugated nation, as an oppressed and subjugated land which had become the victim of violence. It was one of the most significant acts of resistance on a pan-European scale, it was an act which had a significant influence on the decision to recognise our government in exile, it was an act which had much to do with the fact that we finished the war as a victorious state and not a defeated one. This deserves to be fully recognised, because if today we are truly and fully free, then it is thanks to those men and to the victims that the assassination cost us'.

I offer this small book as a modest tribute to all those courageous men, known and unknown, who were prepared to offer up their lives in the fight against the obscene evil personified by Reinhard Heydrich, the Butcher of Prague. When all are gone their brave deeds will live on.

Appendix 1

**Disposition of Czechoslovak Brigade Units
in Warwickshire 1941**

Warwick ○   ○ <u>Leamington Spa</u>

○ <u>Barford</u>

○ <u>Umberslade Manor</u>

○ <u>Moreton Hall</u>

○ <u>Moreton Paddox</u>

○ <u>Wellesbourne</u>

Stratford-upon-Avon ○

○ <u>Walton Hall</u>

○ <u>Friz Hill</u>

○ <u>Kineton</u>

○ <u>Butlers Marston</u>

Not to scale

The Czechoslovak Independent Brigade – Order of Battle and locations of units in Warwickshire, October 1940 – May 1942

Brigade Headquarters, Harrington House, Newbold Terrace, Leamington Spa

Cdr	Brig Gen.	Miroslav-Neuman
A D C	Liet.	Turek
Chief of Staff	Lieut. Col.	Lukas
G	Major	Souhrada
I	Capt.	Krcek
Q	Major	Schweitzer
A	Capt.	Bauer
Supply	Major	Zapletal
Medical	Capt.	Janca

Provost	Capt.	Divoky
Signals	Lieut.	Prachar
Liaison Officers	Major	Prochazka
	Capt.	Nevrala
	Lieut.	Pollak

1st Battalion, Moreton Paddox House

Cdr	Lieut.Col.	Barovsky
2nd i/c	Major	Chermak
Adjt.	Capt.	Dolechek
I O	Lieut.	Cherny

2nd Battalion, Walton Hall, Wellesbourne

Cdr	Liet. Col.	Prikryl
2nd i/c	Major	Sheda
Adjt.	Capt.	Chlup
I O	Lieut.	Horky

3rd Battalion (Cadre only)

Cdr.	Liet. Col.	Sartorie
Adjt.	Capt.	Kubin

Field Artillery Regiment (Two batteries each of four x 75mm) Moreton Hall, Moreton Morrell

Cdr.	Col.	Liska
2nd i/c	Liet. Col.	Husinecky
Battery Cdr. 1	Capt.	Raymond
Battery Cdr. 2	Capt.	Sterba

Anti Tank Battery (Twelve guns completely mobile) The Manor House, Butlers Marston

Cdr.	Lieut. Col.	Kratky
2nd i/c	Lieut. Col	Babatka

Brigade Train (Completely mobile. Equivalent Inde. Bde. Gp R A S C) Stables block, Moreton Hall

Cdr	Major	Blavic

Machine Gun Company (Completely mobile 4 companies each of 4 heavy M/G's)
Woodley House, Warwick Road, Kineton

Cdr.	Lieut. Col.	Novak
2nd i/c	Major	Vovek

Engineer Section, (Mobile) Friz Hill House, Walton

Cdr.	Major	Souhrada
2nd i/c	Capt.	Janousek

Field Ambulance, 19 The Parade, Leamington Spa

Cdr.	Capt.	Janca
2nd i/c	1st Lt.	Heyduck

Reconnaissance Unit, Umberslade Manor

Cdr.	St/Capt.	Solansky
2nd i/c	St/Capt.	Ridky

No 22 Liaison Headquarters, Barford Hill House, Barford

Cdr.	Colonel	Pollock
G S O II	Major	Fillingham MC, DLI
I O	Capt.	Barker (Intelligence Corps)
S C	Capt.	Hart (Royal Fusiliers)
R A S C	Capt.	Griggs
D A D M S	Vacant	

Appendix 2

Burial places of Czechoslovak soldiers who died whilst based in Warwickshire

Graves in the military section of Stratford-on-Avon Cemetery, Evesham Road

JOSEF FLANEK	L/Cpl	11.7.1903 – 25.4.1942
JOSEF HUDEC	L/Cpl	1.12.1911 – 6.7.1941
ZDENEK NOVOSAD	Private	11.8.1918 – 14.11.1941
ANTONIN VORACEK	Private	27.12.1913 – 3.12.1940

Grave in the military section of Leamington Spa Cemetery, Brunswick Street

BOHUMIL CHODORA	Sgt.	16.11.1900 – 27.4.1942

Graves in the Birmingham Jewish Cemetery

KURT GRUNWALD	Private	Died 10.10.1941
FRANTISEK WILHELM	Private	Died 26.11.1941

Lodge Hill Cemetery, Birmingham (Crematorium)

FRANTISEK DALECKY	Capt.	Died 24.12.1940

Grave in St Peter's churchyard, Wellesbourne

STANISLAV PROCHAZKA	Private	13.11.1898 – 29.03.1941

Appendix 3
SOE Parachute Groups sent out by the Czechoslovak Brigade whilst based in Warwickshire

BENJAMIN (16 April 1941)
A single-agent team of **Otmar Reidl** sent to take radio codes & crystals for local resistance groups. Due to a navigation error Reidl was dropped by mistake in Austria and was arrested whilst crossing the border into the Protectorate.

PERCENTAGE (3/4 October 1941)
A single-agent team of **Frantisek Pavelka** (2nd Btn Walton Hall) sent to take a new transmitter and ciphers. He was captured by the Gestapo, sentenced to death by the Berlin People's Court and executed in Plotzensee prison.

ANTHROPOID (28/29 December 1941)
Two-man team to assassinate Reinhard Heydrich. The original team comprised **Josef Gabcik** (1st Btn. Moreton Paddox), and **Karel Svoboda** (2nd Btn. Walton Hall). Svoboda was injured during training and was replaced by **Jan Kubis** (1st Btn. Moreton Paddox). Gabcik and Kubis both committed suicide in the siege of Karel Boromejsky Church crypt 18 June 1942. Svoboda was one of the members of operation drop WOLFRAM later in the war and although he was captured by the Gestapo and imprisoned in Flossenburg concentration camp, he survived the war.

SILVER A (28/29 December 1941)
A three-man team who were tasked with making contact with agent A 54 (Paul Thummel) and establishing an intelligence network prior to subsequent air drops. **Josef Valcik** (2nd Btn. Walton Hall) committed suicide in the crypt at Karel Boromejsky on 18 June 1942. **Alfred Bartos** (2nd Btn. Walton Hall) was arrested in Pardubice on 21 June 1941 and fatally wounded after a gun battle with the Gestapo. Jiri Potucek the team's radio operator was murdered in his sleep by a Protectorate Gendarme on 2 July 1942 whilst on the run from the Gestapo.

SILVER B (28/29 December 1941)
Two-man team of **Jan Zemek** and **Vladimir Skacha** (2nd Btn. Walton Hall) to deliver a transmitter to the underground and to arrange supply drops. The operation had to be abandoned after the jump when the parachuted equipment was lost. Zemek joined local guerrillas and survived the war. Skacha was arrested by the Gestapo and imprisoned in a concentration camp – he survived the war and died in Canada in the mid 1980's.

ZINC (28/29 March 1942)
A three-man team to back up SILVER A and to establish an intelligence network. They also carried a large quantity of money for the resistance. **Arnost Miks** (1st Btn. Moreton Paddox) was shot dead by Czech police while picking up equipment in the Krivorlat forest on the night of 30 April/1 May 1942. Oldrich Pechal (Machine Gun Company, Kineton) was arrested on 2 June 1942 after shooting two German customs officers. He was sentenced to death and executed in Mauthausen on 22 September 1942. Viliam Gerik (2nd Btn. Walton Hall) surrendered to Czech police in Prague on 4 April 1942. He became a Gestapo collaborator and was executed for treason in Dachau on 22 April 1947.

OUT DISTANCE (28/29 March 1942)
A three-man team sent to plant a 'Rebecca' radio beacon to guide RAF bombers to the Skoda works at Pilzen. **Ivan Kolarik** (1st Btn. Moreton Paddox) was arrested by the Gestapo in Brno on 1 April 1942 and committed suicide. He was the first Czechoslovak parachutist to die in the Protectorate. **Adolf Opalka** (Machine Gun Company, Kineton) committed suicide in the Karel Boromejsky crypt 18 June 1942. **Karel Curda** (Automobile Company, Moreton Hall) surrendered to the Gestapo on 16 June 1942 and betrayed his colleagues. Was sentenced to death for treason after the war and was hanged on the same day as Viliam Gerik.

BIVOUAC (27/28 April 1942)

A three-man team whose mission was to sabotage railway bridges and signals at Prerov and the power station at Brno. **Jindrich Coupek** was arrested by the Gestapo and was executed at Mauthausen on 22 September 1944. **Libor Zapletal** was arrested by the Gestapo and executed at Mauthausen on 27 September 1944. **Frantisek Pospisil** was arrested by the Gestapo and executed in Terezin in late 1944.

BIOSCOP (27/28 April 1942)

Three-man team to sabotage the railway bridge at Hradnice and a transformer station at Vsetin. The group's buried material was discovered by the Germans. **Bohuslav Kouba** was arrested on 2 May 1942 and committed suicide by poisoning in his cell at the Police Station in Kutna Hora. **Jan Hruby** died in the siege at the Karel Boromejsky church on 18 June 1942. **Josef Bublik** also died in the Karel Boromejsky church siege on 18 June 1942.

STEEL (27/28 April 1942)

A one man communications team. **Oldrich Dvorak** (1st Btn. Moreton Paddox) was sent out to deliver a new transmitter, spare crystals and poison capsules for the 'Silver A' team. The transmitter which had been hidden in a field was discovered the next day. Dvorak was shot and killed on 10 July 1942 whilst on the run at Radosovice and trying to get back to his family in Slovakia.

INTRANSITIVE (29/30 April 1942)

A three-man team to sabotage the oil refinery at Kolin. **Vojtech Lukastik** was shot dead at Janovice on 8 January 1943 in a skirmish with the Gestapo. **Vaclav Kindl** was arrested in March 1943 and collaborated with the Gestapo. He was accidentally shot dead by a Gestapo member on 20 May 1944. **Bohuslav Grabovsky** was arrested in March 1943 and collaborated with the Gestapo. He was sent to the concentration camp at Terezin and was executed there in October 1944.

TIN (29/30 April 1942)

Two-man team sent out to assassinate Emanuel Moravec the Minister of Education & Propaganda in the Protectorate Government. All of their equipment was lost on landing. **Jaroslav Svarc** died in the Karel Boromejsky church crypt on 18 June 1942. **Ludvik Cupal** shot himself dead on 15 January 1943 in Velehrad during a Gestapo attempt to arrest him.

ANTIMONY (23/24 October 1942)

Three-man radio group to re-establish contact with the home army and to ascertain the fate of the SILVER A team. **Frantisek Zavorka** and **Lubomir Jasinek** both committed suicide in January 1943. **Stanislav Srazil** collaborated with the Germans after being tracked down with the help of Karel Curda (ex OUT DISTANCE)

Bibliography

AUTHOR	TITLE	PUBLISHER
Atherton, Louise	SOE Operations in Central Europe: A guide to the Records in the Public Record Office	PRO
Baumgarten, Henry	Memoirs of a Volunteer	Book Guild, 1990
Burgess, Alan	Seven Men at Daybreak	Dutton, 1960
Burian, Knizek, et al	Assassination : Operation Anthropoid 1941 – 1942	Czech MOD, 2002
Clark, Freddie	Agents by Moonlight	Tempus, 1999
Cowdery, Ray & Vodenka, P	Reinhard Heydrich Assassination	USM Inc., 1984
Hutak, J B,	With Blood and with Iron : The Lidice story	Robert Hale, 1957
Ivanov, Miroslav	Target Heydrich	Macmillan, 1972
Machacek, Karel	Escape to England	Book Guild
Macdonald, Callum	The Killing of SS Obergruppenfuhrer Reinhard Hedrich	The Free Press, 1989
Mackenzie, William	The Secret History of SOE	St Ermin's Press, 2000
Moravec, General	Master of Spies	Bodley Head, 1975
Miller, Russell	Behind the lines : The oral history of Special Operations in World War II	Secker & Warburg, 2002
Stafford, David	Secret Agent : The True story of the Special Operations Executive	BBC London, 2000
Tausky, Margaret	Vilem Tausky tells his story	Stainer & Bell, 1979
Weiner, Jan	The Assassination of Heydrich	Grossman, 1969
West, Nigel	Secret War : The story of SOE	Hodder & Stoughton, 1992
White, Lewis M (Editor)	On All Fronts : Czechs and Slovaks in World War II	East European Monographs, 1991
Articles	After the Battle magazine no 24 1979 (pp3 – 34)	